Difficult
Conversations

Difficult Conversations

What to say in tricky situations without ruining the relationship

Anne Dickson

PIATKUS

Copyright © 2004 by Anne Dickson

First published in 2004 by
Piatkus Books Limited
5 Windmill Street
London W1T 2JA
e-mail: info@piatkus.co.uk

This edition published 2006

The moral right of the author has been asserted

A catalogue record for this book is available from the British Library

ISBN 0 7499 2675 9

Edited by Carol Franklin
Text design by Paul Saunders
Cartoons by Nik Scott, www.nikscott.com

This book has been printed on paper manufactured with respect for the
environment using wood from managed sustainable resources

Typeset by Action Publishing Technology, Gloucester
Printed and bound in Great Britain by Mackays Ltd, Chatham, Kent

This book is dedicated with love to
Madeleine
and
Anne Marie
and
to the memory of
Yvette

Contents

Contents

Introduction

A few years ago, I was engaged in long-term training of women managers within a large hospital that was in the process of merging with another similar sized hospital in the same city. We met together every three weeks. I arrived for our fourth session to find the group members in a state of shock and disarray. The personnel director, Penny, who had been responsible for setting up this particular course on personal development, had been fired that very morning.

How had this event been communicated to her? Penny had arrived for work as usual and entered her office to find her desk had been removed, with its contents in a pile on the floor. She phoned her immediate boss to find out what was happening but he wasn't available! It was only from his secretary that Penny could get a few clues as to what had happened, but no information was given to her officially.

Such shock tactics are not unusual.

We hear of contracts being terminated by e-mail or even by a brief text message; of employees being fired while away on holiday; of others, like Penny, being informed indirectly through the disappearance of their office furniture or even finding empty black bin bags left as an ominous messages on their desks!

The culture within many organisations promotes such abusive behaviour. The characteristics of the culture are the avoidance of direct communication and the total absence of any concern for the individual as *a human being*. People are treated as objects within a vast impersonal machine, to be hired, fired, used, abused, owned, disowned as suits the operators of the machine. Consideration of an employee as a human being entails seeing not a one-dimensional cog but a sentient individual with needs, opinions, feelings and sensitivities.

The avoidance of directness has become an established custom not only in the workplace but in our personal lives as well. It's one of the first stumbling blocks to any possibility of establishing clear communication in all our relationships. People will sit around gossiping or complaining about the behaviour of a family member, friend or acquaintance but wouldn't dream of saying anything directly to that individual. Why not? Because they don't want an argument. They wouldn't want to hurt anybody's feelings.

Basically it's because we feel afraid of anything direct. We feel awkward and uncomfortable or occasionally sorry for the person concerned. Often we feel so resentful, having piled up such a backlog of grievance that we daren't open our mouths for fear of what we may say in the heat of the moment.

At some time in our lives every one of us faces the need to speak up in difficult situations. It may be telling your parents you're not coming home at Christmas for the first time or explaining to a friend or relative that you don't want to go on holiday with them as you have done for many years. Won't they be terribly hurt because you're rejecting them? Or how can you get across to your husband that you hate him driving fast because *he* always retorts that he's not driving dangerously and it invariably ends in a row?

Perhaps you don't know how to tell your boyfriend that you really don't want his best mate coming to live with you both, even if it is only for six months. Won't he think you're being unfair to his friend? Or you may be at your wits end trying to get your children to clear their rooms or share domestic chores because they don't seem to hear you. As a manager you may wonder what's the best way to tell a member of your sales team that he is not meeting his targets and that his job is on the line. And how do you dare ask your boss to improve his way of communicating with you when you're only a junior member of staff?

When a particular topic of conversation is difficult for any reason, we struggle. Despite professional competence, doctors are often only able to inform patients (and their relatives) of a terminal condition in a clumsy and insensitive manner. Managers give employees structured criticism of their performance, unaware that their manner has a hurtful and often devastating effect. At a personal level, we often don't know how to challenge an upsetting pattern of behaviour in a way that the other person can hear. I've witnessed many individuals criticising their partners, parents, children or friends with unwitting condescension and superiority, and then being genuinely amazed and horrified at the aggressive response that comes back at them.

Things often deteriorate, unpleasant things are uttered and rifts appear that last for days or weeks, sometimes causing irreparable breakdown in a relationship. It's small wonder we come to *dread* confrontation. This is usually the word we associate with any encounter that leads to conflict. We antici-pate that to speak up and be direct will lead to arguments, and we don't want the emotional and physical stress that these rows inevitably cause us.

Instead, we keep quiet. We tiptoe around situations, swal-low back our irritation and hurt. We moan or bitch or complain – indirectly. We avoid asking up front for what we want. We manipulate others, trying to get them to do *what* we want *in the way* that we want without the risk of saying anything directly. We ruminate privately or publicly, wishing we could say something or do something. We nag. We moan. At some point, our level of tolerance breaks down and it is then that we resort to aggression in one of its many forms.

What is common to both personal or professional interac-tions is the apparent inevitability of aggression – direct and indirect – in our struggle to communicate our point of view. Most of the time, we have no idea we're being aggressive because we're not shouting or screaming: this is the behaviour we associate with aggression. What characterises aggression, though, is first, an absence of concern for the other person as we bulldoze across others' boundaries in an attempt to combat their intransigence. Secondly, we hurt others: we cause injury with our comments and actions.

Most of us remember occasions when we've wounded oth-ers by what we've said. A lot of the time, we wish we hadn't been hurtful. It's rarely due to any inherent, sadistic enjoyment of causing others pain. We come out with all sorts of comments in what we consider to be self-defence. That's the sequence of aggression: a 'civilised' conversation easily degenerates into a fight. And it's this battleground scenario that we often want to avoid because few of us enjoy this arena. We don't feel equipped to do battle. Some people, it's true, seem to thrive on aggressive interaction, on constant interpersonal war, but not the majority. Most of us find it exhausting, unpleasant and dispiriting.

So if we don't want to take that route, what do we do instead? We can try and say something and risk an unpleasant outcome or we can keep quiet, bury our heads in the sand, deny what's going on, sweep everything under the carpet and wish it would all go away!

Another option is to learn about a different kind of communication: a way of communicating rooted in genuine confidence and a sense of equality with the other person. Imagine having the confidence to be honest with someone without punishing them. Imagine being able to say what you think and feel, and being able to express a difference of opinion without getting into an argument. Imagine being able to ask someone to behave differently or to change a hurtful pattern of behaviour: getting someone to co-operate more fully and get a job actually done on time ... without generating ill feeling.

No, this isn't fairyland! For over two decades, I have been teaching these particular skills. They are surprising, simple and effective, but they require a shift in mental attitude. They require us to challenge some ingrained habits and assumptions, and open our eyes to other ways of seeing.

At the heart of this approach are two concepts: the first is seeing and respecting others as equals and the second is personal power. Personal power means interacting with others from a base of genuine confidence: confidence grounded in self-trust and honesty rather than any pre-packaged image we feel the need to convey to other people. The challenge of this approach is making a genuine commitment to eschew the use of aggression.

There is no magic wand, of course, but it is the purpose and intent of this book to teach you how it is possible, in reality, to be able to express your feelings more honestly to someone you care about *without* it escalating into a row. You can learn how to criticise someone senior to yourself without being punished; how to confront someone junior to you without being resented. You can discover a new and different way of communicating things that are difficult to say, whenever you need to broach potentially explosive topics or are approaching an encounter when you have a request to make that you're feeling nervous about.

The guidelines to this approach are relevant to all aspects of direct communication within our relationships. They apply to direct dialogue, either face to face or over the telephone, but not to written correspondence. In writing, even a clear criticism has a greater impact. This has something to do with it being more impersonal, with written words being more permanent and also more open to misunderstanding because we don't actually hear the tone of voice in which the words are delivered.

E-mail has the advantage of being easy, quick and convenient but it often allows us to avoid dealing with a *direct* response when we don't want to deal with it. Receiving important information or criticism via e-mail often has a shattering effect precisely because we have no way of responding effectively. This is why e-mail offers such a convenient way of avoiding responsibility.

A further point: these are always private interactions and should *never* take place in public. A public arena immediately gives the upper hand to the criticiser and therefore makes equality totally impossible: the other party will feel accused, however reasonable the content and tone of the criticism, and will respond accordingly.

... easy, quick and convenient

The focus of the book is on direct and spoken communication: precisely that area so many of us would prefer to avoid. Whether you have difficult things to say to your children, your parents, your friends, your employers or subordinates, your neighbours, colleagues or your partners, this book is your guide. It is a guide to communicating without aggression, being authoritative without being oppressive. Knowing how to communicate clearly and more effectively helps us to be direct within all our relationships without damaging them.

Part 1

The theory

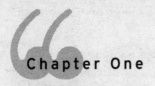

Chapter One

Will I win or will I lose?

What actually makes what we have to say *difficult*? Some topics of conversation, such as sex or money, we all tend to find difficult, but most of the time, what makes something difficult is that we anticipate *trouble*. We anticipate that what we have to say will be met by resistance and possibly hostility or that our words will cause hurt and disappointment. This is mainly why something becomes difficult. We then see ahead the inevitability of a conflict between our needs and feelings and those of someone else. It is this anticipation of conflict that is so crucial because at that moment, in our minds, usually without our realising it, a process is set in motion.

Whenever we ruminate about the possibility of criticising someone or consider bringing up a delicate or tricky topic of conversation, we will generate, in our minds, concerns and anxieties about the outcome. Will it work? Will they listen? How will it affect our relationship? What will they think of me? Am I going to open up a can of worms? Am I laying myself open to attack?

Depending on how we *see* our relationship to the other person, we begin, in our imagination, to estimate our chances. In order to see whether it is going to be worth making the effort of communication, we assess the likelihood of a favourable outcome. The prospect of confrontation makes us anxious and, in our anxiety, our imagination narrows the field to just two possibilities of outcome: winning or losing. So we weigh up the odds of a favourable outcome (winning) and what we use to measure these odds are measures of *power*.

You may be totally unaware that this process is taking place. But it is and how we know it exists is because it emerges in our attitudes and behaviour. Whenever you imagine a situation where you need to confront someone or communicate something you feel awkward about, you'll find various doubts and concerns going through your mind, each of them undermining your resolve to speak up.

See how many of the common concerns below you recognise:

● They might get cross

● They might take offence

● I'll get into trouble

● I can't say that to the boss!

● It'll get nasty

● I might be wrong

● She won't like me any more

● There'll be awful repercussions

● It'll end up with him shouting at me

● There's no point because they won't listen

Or these . . .

- He can't help it
- None of us is perfect . . . we all have our faults don't we?
- She's having a very difficult time as it is
- He's too old for me to say anything
- She's too young and inexperienced
- He's only got one leg
- She doesn't know she's doing it
- He's too fragile
- They'd be shattered
- You just feel sorry for them really

These two lists broadly reflect our own perspective of where we stand in relation to the other person. The first group of anxieties reflects the anticipation of a failed outcome because we see the other person as more powerful than ourselves. We fear not being listened to, being disliked, possibly the target of a retaliatory attack.

The second group reflects the reverse: a sense of having more power and the other person being correspondingly weaker. Therefore our concerns centre around the other's inability to cope with what we would like to say to them. Without realising what we're doing, we adopt the mindset of feeling superior to other mere mortals, judging them as simply inadequate and therefore lacking the ability to comprehend or change: so why bother?

Read the two lists again and see if you can pick up the tones of the 'lower' position of the first voice, looking up, and the 'higher' position of the second voice, looking down.

These concerns are familiar and play a major role in dissuading us from dealing with problems directly. We convince ourselves that we will be unheard or punished; that the other person will be devastated. This conviction keeps us from speaking up when we would like to because we are *always* alert to the ever-present possibility of aggression. Why does aggression seem so inevitable?

Difficult conversations, as I said earlier, are those in which we anticipate trouble. We anticipate trouble because we anticipate conflict. Confrontation – the meeting of two opposing points of view or needs or feelings – is the umbrella term for such conversations. It includes giving criticism or delivering bad news because we assume, rightly, that the other person is not exactly going to be delighted to hear what we have to say. Any interaction, which puts us in some kind of opposition to someone else, generates anxiety. We imagine what might happen and our imagination is very strongly influenced by what we have already experienced directly or witnessed indirectly. Past experience has taught us that confrontation means aggression, so much so that we find it impossible to imagine anything different.

All our anxieties about any kind of confrontational situation reveal the subconscious association of confrontation as a weapon. Of course, confrontation and criticism can be a means of attack, sometimes causing a great deal of permanent emotional and physical damage. We have all experienced this, as children and as adults, to a greater or lesser degree. Therefore, when we are in positions of authority or we feel somehow more powerful, we are often concerned that the consequences of speaking directly will automatically be hurtful. When we're in the 'lower' position, and therefore less powerful, we fear automatically for our *own* safety and survival. It is both a surprise and relief to discover that although criticism has the potential to be harmful, it need not be. As we'll see later on, it depends entirely on the manner and circumstances of its delivery.

The sledgehammer

Before we can learn to separate criticism from aggression and build an alternative approach, we have to identify the current approach to which we are exposed continuously and which is reinforced over and over again in every area of life. This image of confrontation I characterise by a picture of a sledgehammer. This is an image of something heavy, intrusive, hurtful, often abusive. Its use gives rise to the popular 'hit and run' strategy: get them when they least expect it, then disappear to avoid any trouble. The use of sledgehammers isn't always loud and obvious. The removal of someone's desk to indicate termination of employment doesn't make a lot of noise but the impact is no less violent. Sledgehammers can even come wrapped in velvet and embellished with a large bow. Delivery accompanied by a sweet smile and a gentle tone of voice, however, is no less devastating in its impact than when accompanied by a loud tirade of expletives.

The pussyfoot

The awareness of the sledgehammer and our dread of its appearance make us hesitate to speak up and encourage us towards avoidance of direct confrontation of the issue. This approach is characterised by the image of a pussyfoot. We tiptoe around the edges, afraid to cause trouble or rock the boat by being direct and up front. We talk around a subject, alluding perhaps to the cause of concern, hoping desperately that the other person will get the hint and intuitively go into self-correction mode to take the problem away.

What connects the two approaches is the process of *accumulation*. Hesitation and keeping quiet lead to prevarication. Prevarication encourages the collection of small piles of what I call 'pebbles': each representing an individual incident of unexpressed resentment, irritation, hurt, anxiety or fury. These piles accumulate over time. Sometimes incidents assume the proportion of large stones, even the odd boulder, to add to the pile. When the pile is of a sufficient size, it will eventually cause a small (or large) avalanche: the pussyfoot is always the precursor of the sledgehammer.

The first time your friend is late for lunch, you're a bit irritated but let it go. The second time she's late, you're annoyed but keep quiet. The third time, you find yourself getting tense and, as the time goes by, you start getting resentful. You don't say anything when she arrives (*finally!*), but appear a bit curt and withdrawn and when she asks what's wrong, you shrug your shoulders and say 'It's nothing, probably hormonal'. The fourth time, you're counting the minutes she keeps you waiting, one by one, building yourself up to a grand showdown. Your friend arrives with her usual breezy apologies to encounter a towering wall of hostility. She gets defensive in order to protect herself and wham ... you then 'let her have it' with all the amassed fury of the past weeks.

At the moment of avalanche, because we don't know of any alternative, we reach for the sledgehammer. We let our 'self-righteous' anger build up to a point at which we have 'no choice' but to do anything other than speak out. Aggression, loud or soft, overt or indirect, will be always be the weapon nearest to hand. We dredge up old and ancient injuries, blame others for causing all our woes, find chinks in their own emotional armour through which we can inflict a few wounds of our own in retaliation: anything, anything to emerge as the self-righteous and injured winner in this battle.

The intention of the following chapters is to show you how you can learn to speak up and be direct, how you can be critical or negotiate your way through a conflict without resorting to either of these two traditional models. But because we have all been so conditioned by experience of aggression to fear that direct, honest communication is *automatically* harmful, we have first to dig a little deeper and expose the roots of this assumption. We have to understand more clearly about the nature of power.

Chapter Two

The usual definition of power

We live, in this world, within a structure of power, which is so familiar that we take its existence for granted. It is all around us, invisible like the air we breathe, and yet it governs our relationships. It affects how we see and what we feel towards each other, and consequently how we interact with all the individuals in our lives.

Perpendicular power

This structure of power is best imaged by a ladder because a ladder represents the linear movement – up and down – along different stages or rungs related to how much power anyone has at any given time. We learn from this image of a ladder that movement is restricted to up or down. We also learn to see others not as equals, but as higher or lower than ourselves.

This structure is very clear in the workplace. Job title is the first demarcation of the position of power within the organisation, an indicator of who is above you or below you on the ladder, or on the same rung. Power is measured in level of remuneration, perks, size of desk and support staff and other trappings of power, the rationale being that this is in exchange for greater responsibility and accountability, even though this isn't always true in practice.

The up/down ladder system filters through into every facet of life. Knowingly and unknowingly, we are constantly mentally assessing or at least aware of our position, our 'power' in relation to others. I call this *perpendicular* power as it is always measured on an up/down scale.

Where does perpendicular power come from? We can divide the sources into four categories: legitimate power, resources, expertise and charisma.

Legitimate power

Legitimate power describes any power that is conferred through the laws or social arrangements of the culture in which we live. Whether a king (over a kingdom), a parent (over a child), a manager (over a department) or a teacher (over a class), this aspect of power stems from our many professional and social roles. It refers to the status and responsibility that comes with a job or particular appointment or general role: head of the family, captain of the team, chairman of the committee. We all experience having this kind of power over others at times and also others having this power over us.

Resources

Power comes from what we own or at least have access to, giving us power over those who don't. Resources range from financial wealth, to weapons, to access to key information, as well as natural resources such as oil, water or diamonds.

Whether you're an executive with a private jet, a teenager with a car or a schoolchild with the most tradeable lunchbox, resources give you power over others. Once again, this kind of power is measured in terms of higher or lower: powerful when we have and powerless when we have not.

Expertise

If you have knowledge and skill that someone else needs but doesn't have access to themselves, you have power over them. If you are the only person who knows the route home when everyone else is lost, you find yourself with this kind of power. When you can articulate what others can't, you again possess this power. Anyone with any expertise who is currently in demand will have a measure of this kind of power over those who don't.

Charisma

This is more difficult to define than absolute wealth or legitimate authority, but is nevertheless a crucial aspect of perpendicular power. Charisma can derive from charm, moral integrity or holiness, a personal presence that makes a profound impression on others. It can also be manufactured charisma, as with the cult of celebrity, the product of hype and publicity machines, imbuing stars of sport and stage and screen with a larger than life magnetic appeal.

Whatever its source, charisma certainly exerts a strong power over others who seek to imitate in appearance or behaviour or achievement. We want to look, sing, cook or dress like those who manifest this kind of power. In more extreme instances, we are seduced into giving our money, our votes and even our lives to follow charismatic individuals, should this be what they demand of us.

The view from the ladder

This up/down system of measuring power affects all our interactions but never more so than when we have to deal with any kind of conflict. Almost without knowing it, we have absorbed the structure of perpendicular power in our minds and hearts so that publicly and, more crucially, privately, it dominates our relationships. It is important, therefore, to bring this into the open, so we can understand how much it affects us.

What happens when we want to ask someone to change his or her behaviour and we only have perpendicular power as a reference point?

For a start, most of us need to believe we're right (i.e. on a higher rung) to confront someone. We anticipate confrontation as a battle and, in order to win, we have to be in a superior position. This will always entail the use of some kind of aggression. Let's take this first example.

▶ MAGGIE AND RICK

Maggie has returned home after work and found her son, Rick, has once again left his breakfast things on the table despite having been told a hundred times to put things in the dishwasher. Rick is 18. Over the next couple of hours, she considers the problem. Yes, he's 18 but he's still her son and should still do as she asks (legitimate power 'over' as a parent but weakened by knowing he is no longer a child). She's out all day, working hard for everyone and has a right to ask (building a strong position of justification through self-righteousness). In fact, she has asked so many times and is sick of being accused of nagging which she wouldn't have to do if he'd just do what she asked (reinforcing her 'over' position with a strong sense of grievance).

When Rick comes in, he senses his mother is in a mood and asks her what's wrong.

> Maggie: 'What's wrong, Rick, is that I came in after work and found your bowl and mug from breakfast still where they were on the table.' (Her face assumes a pained expression.)

> Rick: (sighs) 'Here we go again.' (He makes for the kitchen door.)

> Maggie: 'Don't just walk out like that. Why is it so hard for you to do what I ask? I'm not asking much, you know.' (Attempt at coercion from her upper position through the 'reasonableness' of her request.)

> Rick: 'Mum, look we've been through all this before. I can't stand being nagged.'

> Maggie: 'I'm not nagging' (though she knows she is), 'I'm quite entitled ('over' position) to ask you to contribute to the chores. You're supposed to be grown up now.' (Indirectly aggressive put down.)

> Rick: 'Is it really such a big deal?', (pushed to defend his own position because to agree now would mean he would be the loser), 'Sometimes I just forget. There's a lot more important things in life than washing up, you know. Well, there are in my life anyway.' (Defensive swipe of aggression in retaliation.)

> Exits.

Maggie feels powerless. She's lost the battle.

It's difficult for any of us not to enter a confrontation – which is usually a situation when we want to give a criticism, or ask someone to behave differently – without it taking on the shape of war. This narrow range of alternatives between winning or losing is a result of seeing an encounter in this way. The other evident consequence is that the only weapon we have is aggression. This is a direct consequence of relying solely on access to perpendicular power.

Habituation to life on the ladder has left us alert to the perils of being the loser, i.e. in the lower position. We have all experienced powerlessness, in this sense, being rejected, mocked, excluded, intimidated, ignored or bullied. Whether it's our families, teachers, institutional power or organisational oppression, we're unlikely to escape the experience of what it feels like to be power*less* in the hands of others and at their mercy.

This experience determines our most familiar starting point when broaching any kind of confrontational situation. Remember, this includes any encounter where we expect to find ourselves at odds with the other person: when this occurs we want to guarantee we're going to win. This is why we assume the position of attack. To this end, we build up in our minds an armour of superiority to withstand any counterattack from the other person. When we feel 'justified' in our criticism, it means we have sufficient weaponry on our side: unfortunately this usually means that we don't listen to the other person's point of view. Maggie is caught in a mental trap of her own making, one that traps us all until we can find an alternative. As long as she sees her interaction with Rick on this issue as a battle and approaches it as a battle, she will not learn how to interact with him as both mother to son *and* equal to equal as human beings.

Whenever we are in the upper position on the ladder, as a parent, teacher or employer, it's tempting to use the leverage from our position to deliver the criticism. Because it's our job or our right to do so, we believe we have the upper hand and therefore tend to talk down. The criticism can be effective in that the other person understands all too clearly what is wrong, but this approach always sows seeds of resentment.

ANTONIA AND INGRID

Antonia wants to say something to Ingrid, the au pair. She arrived home from work yesterday as usual at 7 o'clock to find her two small sons still not ready for bed. She feels tired and stretched to the full, managing work and family, and feels very annoyed. Antonia believes she has every right to complain because she employs Ingrid to do a certain job so, for her, the demarcation is clear. Ingrid's paid very well (for what *little* she has to do), she has a really nice room and it's her job, after all, to do what she's told. Having assembled mentally an impressive array of grievances and self-righteous indignation to back up her criticism, Antonia decides to say something before she goes to work the next morning.

Next day, they're in the kitchen, the boys playing, Ingrid preparing their breakfast, Antonia grabbing a quick cup of coffee.

> Antonia: *'By the way, Ingrid, I didn't appreciate coming home last night and finding the boys still not ready for bed. I really have enough on my hands without you not doing your job properly.'(Looks at Ingrid squarely.) 'Do you understand me?'*

Ingrid (apologetically): 'I'm sorry. I forgot about the time.'

Antonia (raising her voice): 'Well, that's simply not a good enough excuse. You're paid to do a job here and I'd like you to do it properly. I don't want to have to tell you.'

Ingrid: 'I've said I'm sorry.'

Antonia (feeling dominant and wanting to reinforce her position of authority): 'And I noticed there were some toys left in the garden overnight last week. I'd have thought you could at least remember to do that . . . What are you giving Toby now, you know he's not meant to have that cereal!'

Ingrid (her voice slightly raised now in self-defence): 'Everything I'm doing is wrong this morning!'

Antonia (indignant): 'Don't you get angry with me! I won't have it. Just remember your position here.'(Looks at the clock.) 'God, I've got to go.' (Goes to kiss the children goodbye.)

Antonia has won the battle in the sense that Ingrid will probably obey the instructions. However, this kind of aggressive interaction is not going to add anything beneficial to the environment in which both Antonia and Ingrid have to live. Operating only from a standpoint of perpendicular power breeds a climate of resentment and tension, which never gets the best out of anybody. This is why, if we want to be direct without damaging our relationships, we have first to acquire a different perspective on perpendicular power. We need to see its limitations, that it is *not* the whole picture but only one part. Secondly, we can learn to become less reliant on it by developing our personal power instead.

Chapter Three

Perpendicular power in perspective

Perpendicular power has four key distinguishing features.

1. The ladder

This kind of power is always measured along the shape of a ladder. You'll experience simultaneously having this kind of power *over* others while also being, in some contexts, power*less*. You have legitimate power over some and are under others; you have more expertise in some areas and less in others, making you, more or less, powerful. Different ladders co-exist in our society: having less money but more expertise than someone, being youthful but less experienced, being less intelligent but far wealthier.

There is nothing inherently wrong in these ladders. They provide a handy system of measurement – like a ruler – which gives us certain useful information. They tell us in a very short time our relative positions and from there we work out how to behave with one another. When it comes to communication, the problem is not that we use the ladders as guidelines but because they've become the *only* guidelines. We've become completely habituated to up/down thinking, rather as if our heads had been restricted to a single up/down nodding movement on our spinal columns. It is the monopoly of this approach that, I believe, causes us a lot of problems and makes it impossible for many of us to communicate more effectively because we concentrate over much on the narrow range of alternatives between being above (winning) or below (losing).

2. A temporary power

It's important to remember that perpendicular power doesn't last for ever. Professional and personal roles come to an end and, when they end, so does access to this form of power. Resources are finite and exhaustible, subject, for instance, to uncontrollable market forces, climate change, political fluctuation. The power of expertise is only relevant when that expertise is needed: social and professional needs change. Celebrity status evaporates with the passing moods of fashion. Physical beauty and prowess are associated with youth – the young (over)/old (under) ladder – and this aspect of power will diminish with the process of time.

3. Dependent on an external source

Perpendicular power is issued by outside agencies: the organisation, the rules of society, cultural norms, fashionable trends of the era. Legitimate, resource and expertise power are both attributed and removed in life independently of any personal character, independent of any personal virtues or vices. Although charisma can emanate from personal characteristics, its actual power is still externally dependent for its existence on the continuing adoration of devotees: no fans – no power.

4. It is arbitrary

Perpendicular power comes our way through no merit of our own. It doesn't matter who you are, what kind of person you are: it is not a question of being deserving or undeserving. Sometimes, you don't even choose this power. It comes with a job or you find it a function of your responsibilities, perhaps even burdensome at times. Charismatic power is also attributed quite independently of any inner moral integrity. Analysis of the secret of an individual's charisma leads just as often to the portrait of a sinner as a saint.

Balancing two kinds of power

Fully understanding the nature of perpendicular power – identifying it, accepting it, enjoying it or regretting it – means you can learn to handle this form of power differently. It helps you realise that when you're in the 'under' position, it isn't because the other person is in any way a better or superior person: so instead of grovelling, you can interact from a more equal standpoint. You learn you can offer a criticism even to someone 'over' you in rank or expertise.

Conversely, the realisation that the person in front of you who is, as it happens, on a lower rung, is not in any way an inferior person, alters your attitude. It shifts your approach and your dialogue into something more parallel. You can learn to manage your legitimate power and authority in a much clearer way, neither neglecting your responsibilities nor oppressing the other person. Seeing someone not only as 'below' you in status or responsibility, but as a fellow human being *as well*, is at the core of treating others as equals within a perpendicular structure.

It can also help to realise just how little real security of power is guaranteed. Despite our best efforts to avoid risk and to be in control of everything, we know deep down that the ladder of perpendicular power is a very insecure place. It's a place of constant movement. We can't stand still even when we get to the rung we're aiming for. We may be intent on an ideal dress size, a dream occupation, a desired partner, a designer kitchen, a state we label happiness ... but when we get there and look up, like the end of the rainbow, there's always another goal to aim for. When we look down, we wobble and worry and hold on tight because we know that, despite our best efforts, we could get knocked off our rung at any time by something we hadn't foreseen: a partner's infidelity; redundancy; sudden injury or onset of illness; collapse of pension funds. Even the more predictable threats to our status can take us by surprise: children leaving home; the process of ageing; being superseded in our expertise.

Acknowledging the temporary nature of this kind of power, *you can learn to let go of it when you have to*. The permanent insecurity of moving up or down the ladder makes it hard to relinquish this power gracefully. This is why we often try to hold on. People resort to being rigidly authoritarian, waging war, having cosmetic surgery, engaging in dishonest and criminal practices, and holding on to worn out relationships precisely because the need to cling to wealth and position and status and significance is so great.

When, on the other hand, you can let go when you need to, you'll probably face inevitable feelings of loss and require a process of readjustment. However, I believe that learning how to let go of this kind of power – whether parental/professional/social – when the time requires, is essential to our physical and mental health. Losing some obvious signs of this power – such as title, salary, work identity/family identity – doesn't always have to spell inevitable failure, simply change.

As long as we're preoccupied exclusively with our own positions on various ladders, fretting about unfavourable comparisons, pitting ourselves against others in a struggle to climb upwards, it's impossible to develop a broader vision. So much emotional energy is spent on comparison and competition or in private self-recrimination for not being as attractive/qualified/academic/sorted/popular or having less social status/less professional kudos/achieved less in life than everyone else.

All you have to do at the moment is get a little distance from the ladders. Acknowledge them but instead of allowing them to take up the *whole* picture, make room in the frame for something else. Create some mental space. The ladders are still there and always will be but once you see them for what they are – simply a temporary structure superimposed to make society more orderly and controllable – you begin to focus on another reality alongside. You can alter your relationship to those ladders without having to change them.

Behind and beyond the ladders lies a different reality, less dependent on the ups and downs of everyday life, a reality that offers a complementary definition of power from a separate source: not from outside the person this time but from within. Once you really see this, an internal process begins, enabling you to interact with other people in an entirely different way. Instead of an exclusive up/down focus, you add an extra dimension of equality. When you do this, your whole approach to communication is literally transformed.

Chapter Four

Personal power

Most of us are already aware of what is called personal power, but it's not easy to find the words to describe it. It becomes eclipsed by the domination of our need for external validation. So what exactly does it mean?

Personal power is different from perpendicular power in that it has nothing to do with external attributes, assets, expertise or status. It has everything to do with a strong sense of self, the ability to balance care for oneself with care for others, the commitment to be true to yourself and the capacity to see beyond the ladders of life.

If I had to choose one word that sums up personal power, it would be the word *congruence*. This word describes a consistency of being, an agreement between what you feel and what you say and how you behave. This is why phrases like being true to yourself, being all you can be, and words like spontaneity and flexibility are often considered aspects of personal power.

Personal power is related to self-esteem in that you regard yourself as you would a dear friend rather than as your worst enemy. But this is self-esteem that comes from truly accepting yourself, with all your frailties as well as your strengths, which distinguishes it from self-esteem that is far more connected to status on the ladder. Confusing self-esteem with aggression (always getting what you want), with denial (hiding vulnerability and weakness), with self-centredness (always putting yourself first) or self-delusion (you can succeed at everything if you want to), has no connection to authentic personal power.

Similarly, personal power is related to confidence but not the kind of confidence that depends on showing a false or manufactured image to hide anxiety: instead it describes a confidence based in acknowledging reality and trusting yourself to deal with that reality as best you can.

Personal power emanates from within a person. When we perceive this in someone, we sometimes call it radiance or compassion, peace or wisdom. We sense the person's inner joy and vitality. It comes across in someone's courage and lack of arrogance and aggression. We get a sense of someone who knows their own limits and is clear about their boundaries; someone who is able to be sufficiently detached from the need for others' approval to speak up and stand alone when necessary.

Features of personal power

Because of its nature, personal power is harder to put into specific categories like perpendicular power but there are certain common features:

Balance

A key aspect of personal power, balance extends to our behaviour and our attitudes. It describes the ability to give an equal value to our own needs and those of others. It helps us balance our wish to reach out with love and also to set clear limits and say no. It helps us negotiate from an equal position instead of automatically seeing a situation of conflict as a struggle for dominance.

Emotional awareness

Emotional awareness requires us to take our feelings seriously enough to assume responsibility for them, instead of denying them or blaming others for causing them. It means identifying what you are feeling and putting this into words. The ability to express clearly when you feel hurt or angry or fearful will become a crucial part of learning to talk through difficult issues without aggression.

Integrity

Integrity is an overused word in our world of spin but it is essential to personal power. It echoes the congruence already mentioned, everything being all of a piece, instead of having one principle in mind but following another in practice. Integrity provides a thread of coherence through all aspects of our lives. The greatest enemy of integrity is denial and dishonesty with oneself. Pretending you don't see or hear or feel what you *do* see and hear and feel undermines personal power more quickly than anything else.

... denial and dishonesty with oneself

Most of us have become so self-conscious and concerned about how we appear to others that our integrity is weakened. Whenever we concentrate more on saying the right thing, making the right impression, second-guessing someone else's response, controlling the outcome of an interaction than what we are actually experiencing *inside*, we lessen our integrity and our power as a consequence.

The main characteristics of perpendicular power – external dependence, arbitrariness, lack of permanence, up/down in measure – can be contrasted with the kind of power we are describing here.

Characteristics of personal power

A continuum

Whereas the symbol for perpendicular power is a ladder, the symbol for personal power is a more of a continuously moving circle. We are constantly involved from birth to death in a continuous process of evolution, shedding, accommodation and change. Instead of seeing the world as arranged in a hierarchy of position, starting at the bottom and ending at the top, operating from a place of personal power helps you to see difference and equality co-existing, everything belonging equally to the whole. You are able to see we are different from each other rather than narrowly defined as inferior or superior. This constitutes a radical departure from our 'normal' way of seeing people higher or lower than ourselves and, as we'll see, will affect our entire approach to communication.

Independent of external status

Equally radical is the fact that personal power exists entirely independent of rank, status, class, achievement, education, gender, background, physical beauty or strength, expertise, health, wealth or even age. This power can be equally evident in the spontaneity and exuberance of a small child as in the wisdom and serenity of an elderly person. The natural compassion that shines out of a relatively inexperienced nurse or the quiet, self-reliant confidence that resides in a man who lives a humble existence speak of a source of power far removed from the expertise and artifice of the higher echelons.

Abiding

Perpendicular power increases and decreases as a direct consequence of external changes. Personal power is more of a constant life energy, enabling us to build a different self-belief alongside the ladder, a self-trust that survives even the lowest points in our lives. I think of it as similar to a lifelong candle flame that can glow or sputter according to how much oxygen is available to feed it.

Although it comes from within, personal power is subject to fluctuations and when we are especially vulnerable, the flame can be small. Yet somehow this inner force remains throughout all the successes and failures, the highs and lows of temporal life. During times of aloneness and despair, suffering and loss, this power is what still stands, independently. When we see adults who survive extreme circumstances intact and emerge uncorrupted by the horrors they've experienced, we realise that it's not so much what happens to us that matters so much as how we respond to what comes our way.

This is the lesson about personal power: it is there all the time but we forget about it. We become too absorbed in our positions on various ladders. We get used to functioning within one frame of reference alone and we lose sight of other possibilities. When it comes to effective communication, clearly, the stronger your personal power, the more able you are to negotiate as an equal. The skills described in the following chapters are all geared to building an awareness of personal power while maintaining whatever power you have on the ladder as well. These skills include initiating a discussion and closing it, speaking through your anxiety instead of being overwhelmed by it, staying on your own path with what you want to convey, while also being able to respond to the person on the receiving end. You can learn how not to give your own power away to others, as when you avoid making clear requests or choices and allow others to do your thinking for you. You may only be trying to be courteous, but this behaviour leaves you at a disadvantage.

Once you realise that certain habitual behaviour is always going to diminish your personal power, you then have the choice whether to continue or to alter it. The most common habit that undermines the ability to communicate effectively is the tendency towards aggression.

Chapter Five

Kicking the habit of aggression

Personal power offers us an extra dimension in which to work. It opens out the narrow option of a battle in which only two outcomes (winner/loser) are possible into a more creative range of possibilities. From this standpoint, it becomes possible to *combine* both kinds of power and, once you learn to do this, you'll find that any interaction, in any part of your life, becomes easier to handle without aggression.

So how do we break a lifetime's habit? How can we put aside the need to win? It is extremely difficult because whenever we don't like what's happening to us, our responses veer automatically towards the aggression. We may react passively for a while, preferring to keep quiet, take it or ignore it. We remain fearful of losing: 'there's no point/there's no way/it won't make any difference'. However, when our feelings reach a certain pitch – at some point, at some time, with someone – we swap to the opposite 'up' position. This can mean a direct attack or a more subtle form of hurtful or vengeful behaviour that establishes us on top.

This seesaw of interaction is so common and so ingrained that it feels like second nature. Aggression is everywhere. It has always been seen as necessary in the arenas of sport or war, and is now applauded and justified in commercial and corporate spheres. We witness aggression on our screens, we encourage it and even reward it. Even if we happen to be personally uncomfortable with aggression, we assume it is natural and inevitable because it's all we've ever known.

The link between anxiety and aggression

Our continuing preoccupation with the loss or retention of perpendicular power is fuelled by constant anxiety. We do not want to be powerless and yet life on the ladder is by its nature insecure. Fear of losing face, putting a foot wrong, appearing vulnerable, being at fault, losing authority, seeming emotional – all aspects we associate with being power*less* – propel us into aggression. Aggression is always born out of fear, *never* out of real confidence or true self-esteem.

The most insidious aspect of all this is that aggression breeds aggression. Hostility felt in response to aggression is stored and, at some time, in some place, the person who has been on the receiving end, made to feel power*less*, will find themselves in the upper position and mete out the same treatment, tasting the fruits of tyranny in their turn. As long as we only look up or down, this rigidity remains. Aggression simply cannot take root in personal power because of the genuine conviction of equality. Winning loses its imperative when you become clear that this is a reciprocal interaction, even when you're the boss and the other is the junior, even when you're the patient and the other is the expert consultant. When demarcations of unequal status are seen alongside the equality of personal power, it changes the picture quite radically. You can put aside your need to show the junior that you're the boss by dominating the discussion or refusing to engage in any kind of consultation. You can make an authoritative request and listen to the reply, knowing that co-operation is better for effective teamwork than mindless coercion. Instead of being resigned to the status of a powerless patient, you can reserve the right to have your questions answered and concerns heard. If you feel in need of support, you can heed your anxiety and take someone along as a supportive presence to your consultation.

What's the alternative?

Once we get down from the ladder, in other words, once we stop worrying about winning and losing for a moment, it's easy to feel a bit disorientated. What direction do we go in if it's not up or down? What do we start from? The answer requires us to commit ourselves to developing a new habit. Even when we are more consciously trying *not* to be aggressive, we still find ourselves reverting to old patterns. They are so embedded in the fabric of human interaction that we seem unable to avoid them.

We can't avoid them, in fact, until we put something else in their place. The guidelines and examples in the rest of this book offer an alternative. They will show how we can best avoid falling into the old traps and discover that once we keep aggression out of our own communication, it has a profound effect on the outcome.

It comes as a total revelation to those who start on this path that we make a big mistake when we attribute someone's aggressive response to a basic aggressive instinct. Nine times out of ten, any aggressive response you get from someone is not an indication of an intrinsically unpleasant quality in *them*: it is a response to something you say or do yourself in the first place.

Although, of course, we are vulnerable to random violence in this world, speaking in terms of most ordinary human interaction, we tend not to be ambushed in this way. In conversation, we mostly get back what we put out. In our tone of voice, body posture and turn of phrase, we emit all sorts of aggressive signals. Most of us don't enjoy aggression but we are rarely aware of how often it infiltrates our communication.

Aggression and anxiety

It happens for two reasons. Most of us are anxious about confrontation of any kind and the image of battle encourages us to psyche ourselves up because we don't want confrontation and we don't want to lose. Our anxiety is not itself a problem. This is a normal response to encountering any kind of conflict. It becomes a problem when our response to anxiety is to *hide* it in order to appear less vulnerable/more fearsome to the enemy. It is this attempt to conceal our anxiety that creates so much miscommunication. Expressed openly, anxiety does no harm. Pushed down, it emerges through all kinds of non-verbal signals that we can't control, but which send out messages to the other person. Attempts to hide anxiety always emerge as defensiveness: these messages trigger in turn an aggressive response. This is how aggression escalates and it is why you'll find becoming more aware of and more comfortable with expressing your feelings so central to personal power.

Chapter Six

A *new approach*

This new approach starts with three basic questions that you have to ask yourself when considering any situation in your life that you'd like to address but feel uneasy about doing so:

- What is happening?

- What do I feel about it?

- What would I like to be different?

These three questions and their answers are absolutely essential. Without them, there is no possibility of assertive confrontation. Aggressive, yes, ineffectual, yes, but not assertive: clear, honest and free of blame. Each of these three questions brings a challenge of their own. If you want to engage with anyone at all, you need the answers to these three questions, not to use them as weapons but as necessary tools for your own survival.

Question One: What is happening?

What is or has the other person been doing? Or not doing? What have they done to upset you? This is where you need to be very clear and specific. What is the behaviour that you object to?

The predominant impulse in most interactions is the wish to blame. This means the focus is entirely on the other person – what they do or don't do, how they should or shouldn't behave, their inadequacies, their faults, their problems. If we're not careful, we end up so preoccupied with these details (which we've often ruminated on for a long time!) that we lose sight of the specific behaviour.

You have to separate the behaviour from the person. Why? Because whenever you give a criticism, the use of labels (e.g. you're stupid/lazy/selfish/incompetent/devious/not to be trusted) is the verbal equivalent of a slap in the face. No matter how you may protest 'It's true, though, he is like that, anyone can tell you . . .', you'll need to avoid labelling someone if you want to avoid setting up a battle scenario.

The tendency is to start with a general complaint:

- My partner gets really aggressive

- My mother keeps treating me like a child

- My secretary's not as careful as she should be

The answer to this first question has to be honed down to a fine point: what is the specific behaviour that upsets you? What precisely is it that you want to be different? What is it they do that you don't like?

These answers then become:

- My partner shouts at me

- My mother makes appointments for me without consulting me

- My secretary doesn't check everything thoroughly

Now you have something specific to work with. Making it specific helps to avoid being judgemental or disapproving, all of which will automatically place you in a superior position. By taking a small step back and asking yourself to be specific, you dismantle the usual strategy of ploughing in with plenty of emotional fuel but absolutely no focus.

Question Two: What do you feel about it?

This is usually a question that people find very difficult to answer because we all find it hard to be specific about our feelings. For all sorts of reasons, we've learned to give more credence to what we think and less to what we feel. So initial answers to this question will often continue to focus on the other person. Instead of expressing your feelings, you find yourself elaborating further on your complaint. If you're feeling less powerful than the other person, this elaboration appears as an excuse for the other's behaviour:

- He's not shouting at *me* really, he just gets overwrought

- She's only trying to be nice, she means well

- She's usually very competent: it's only a small lapse

This approach often undermines your resolve to say anything at all.

On the other hand, if you're feeling superior, you find your comments reflect the higher moral ground on which you've placed yourself:

- He ought to be able to control his temper

- You'd think she'd be able to treat me like an adult by now

- She should be much more conscientious

Approaching someone from the moral high ground comes across as an attack so is best avoided: it's essential to work out what you *feel*, not what you think.

Identifying the appropriate feeling takes practice. Without it, you'll set off automatically concentrating on relative status – who's right and who's wrong – rather than approaching it with an open mind. Personal power is developed by familiarising yourself with your feelings and this means identifying what you're feeling and communicating this. What gets in the way of this apparently simple task? The answer is a lifetime of entrenched attitudes to feelings.

Understanding the importance of feelings

Stand by for another radical shift in thinking. Most of us have incorporated, through lack of adequate emotional education, some very odd and unhelpful myths about feelings:

1. Feelings are either positive or negative. Only the positive ones are socially acceptable.

2. Other people cause our feelings and, if they're negative feelings, they should be blamed for making us suffer.

3. Feelings are childish, messy, uncontrollable and weak.

4. Anyone who bursts into tears inappropriately, in other words beyond the age of 12, should be pitied/given a stiff drink/dispatched to a proper therapist.

5. A funeral is the exception to the above but even then, not for *too* long nor *too* loudly.

6. There is happily a wide range of medication now available, e.g. Ritalin, hormonal replacements, anti-depressants, which can sort out most negative (undesirable and unwelcome) feelings in most people so there's really no excuse for feelings to interfere with normal life.

7. Aggression and anger are identical, acceptable when we want them but unacceptable when we don't. In any case, women shouldn't display either!

8. If we have to have feelings, then it's better to have them within the bosom of our families, but not around people we're not close to, which includes anyone we work with.

9. Feelings are dangerous in that they ambush us when we least expect it and tend to get out of hand so it's better not to mention them at all. Keep the conversation rational and safe.

10. Unless you're talking to a counsellor, of course, then it's acceptable, as long as you just talk. You mustn't give in to feelings and make a fool of yourself by actually starting to blubber or make a scene. Then it just gets messy and everyone gets embarrassed.

Unsurprisingly, therefore, when it comes to the second essential question (what do I feel about it?), we usually have no idea what we're really feeling and, if we do, we're all set to blame the other person for causing this negative state of affairs. This provides us with a useful launching pad for whatever missile we're going to send.

A different view

Imagine now a different view, where you don't see emotion as weaker than reason, where instead of a good/bad hierarchy of feelings, you understand that all feelings are human, whether we like them or not.

Imagine a non-linear approach that taught us that:

- Our emotions are a valuable source of learning both for our individual development and as part of our relationships

- We fear emotions and see them as obstacles to proper functioning only because we haven't learned to see them as potential energy

- Emotions are psychosomatic events, in other words they occur in the mind and body simultaneously so that physical release of emotion is natural and healthy

- It's vital to distinguish between short-term control of emotion, which we all have to learn as part of growing up – like not having a tantrum in an inappropriate context – and the permanent taboo and suppression of all emotional expression, i.e. never being able to express your sorrow or anger, even in private

- Emotions are indicators of normal human experience, not of sickness. They become 'abnormal' only when constantly driven underground to fester

Why are emotions relevant? When it comes to confrontation and criticism, when it comes to speaking up to a family member, a partner, someone at work, a friend or neighbour, the core of our difficulty is that we have feelings. It is precisely because we experience feelings in our relationships that makes them seem problematic. We believe we can manage whatever goes on as long as we can deal with things in a reasonable way. As soon as feelings are stirred up, we don't know how to handle them: feelings equate with problems. We feel undone and afraid, as if we're suddenly in alien territory, hence our difficulty in dealing with certain emotionally charged or awkward situations. Instead of tackling those feelings openly and honestly, we keep them covered up. We pretend not to have certain feelings. We go into battle instead of acknowledging vulnerability.

This is why it is essential in any effective model of confrontation that we include this second question and answer. The expression of what we feel is what makes our dialogue human: otherwise, even with the 'right' words, the approach will not be sincere but merely superficial. Since most of us have been taught to keep feelings well into the background, the task of identifying a feeling is like embarking on a journey through totally alien territory.

A basic emotional map

It is hard, at the beginning, to identify precisely what we are feeling and useful therefore to consider these emotions as falling into one of three categories: anxiety, anger and sadness.

It is helpful to look at each category in turn and get a sense of what you're feeling and why. This is not about analysing your feelings for the sake of it, but, instead, being able to identify and understand them in the context of how you are responding emotionally to someone else's behaviour. The better you know how you tend to respond to certain behaviour, the better chance you'll have of communicating this without needing to punish the other person for making you have feelings you don't know how to deal with.

Anxiety

This is the core of a whole range of feelings from terror to mild uncertainty. It includes alarm, fear, panic, nervousness and bewilderment. These feelings are related to any experience of not belonging, being alone, being unsure of what is happening or is going to happen. It encompasses major events such as being threatened by violence or waiting for the results of a biopsy; it occurs in response to the panic of wondering if your children are safe, speaking in front of a large gathering, afraid of incurring someone's displeasure. Uncertainty about making the right impression, worry about a loved one's health, the unease of walking into an unfamiliar environment: these are all aspects of the same 'family' of feelings.

These feelings arise in response to experiences of uncertainty, insecurity, being unsafe, vulnerable or out of control of what is happening to us. Although we may choose to watch horror movies from the safety of our own homes for the thrill of fear, this is different from the real thing. Part of the attraction of these movies is that it gives us an opportunity to be frightened and scream without censure because the fear we feel is removed from reality: the experience is a fantasy. The real-life experience would be totally different because then we would be genuinely out of control and the resulting fear would be so real that we would be unlikely even to scream: our energies would be entirely directed towards survival.

What we experience physically when fearful or afraid puts the lie to the notion that feelings only happen in the mind. They happen in our bodies, which give us lots of physical signs of emotion. 'Butterflies', nausea, diarrhoea, sweaty skin, palpitations, cool shivers, tight muscles in the stomach, neck or shoulders are some of these indicators.

Anger

This range of feelings includes outrage, fury and frustration, irritation and resentment. Again it encompasses our response to events large and small, significant and insignificant: being patronised or publicly criticised, finding you've been excluded from the information 'loop', the mess in the kitchen, the washing machine breaking down, somebody interrupting your favourite programme. We feel these feelings when we are ignored, when we witness or feel a victim of injustice, cruelty or hypocrisy. It may arise when we are lied to or as a result of the repeated lack of response to a legitimate request. These feelings occur when we have no choice, when our boundaries are transgressed in some way: being mugged or burgled, your mail being read, something you say being taken out of context, a betrayal of a confidence.

Our bodies again indicate when angry feelings are on the rise: heat, sweating, headaches, increased heartbeat, muscular tension in neck, shoulders and jaw, restlessness. If these feelings accumulate momentum, there's often a sensation of excess energy, a felt desire to hit out or shout out or run amuck.

Sadness

This last range of emotions includes our feelings of hurt, loss, sorrow and loneliness. These may occur in response to experiences of rejection, criticism, being excluded from a group, being unloved or disliked. The events in our lives, which deprive us of love and closeness can be major – the grief of separation, the break up of a relationship or the death of a loved one – or minor, as when a holiday ends or you have to say a goodbye. Such feelings arise when someone withdraws from us emotionally or physically or when we find ourselves the butt of someone else's mockery, bullying or continuous criticism; when we feel constantly overlooked and unvalued.

Different bodily sensations occur in response to these feelings: heaviness, coldness, emptiness, lack of appetite and energy, a tightness in the stomach and throat and around the eyes.

Identifying the predominant feeling

Reading through these three groups of emotions, you may be able to identify with the different experiences. Although we tend to experience a mixture of feelings in reality this doesn't matter in terms of communication. It may be that you feel both hurt and angry at someone's criticism of you or afraid and sad in response to intimidation. We don't have to limit ourselves to one feeling only but it is useful when thinking about the answer to this second question – 'How do you feel?' – to identify for yourself the *predominant* feeling. This will give you a starting point from which to begin your conversation.

Emotional arousal

Emotional arousal describes the level at which you feel something. Are you a little bothered, mildly irritated, seething with anger or about to blow a gasket? Learning to include feelings in your communication also entails the whole discipline of emotional management. This means simply developing a degree of awareness about what you're feeling and noticing when the levels of feelings are interfering with your ability to function properly.

You can begin discerning bodily sensations without becoming overly self-conscious. All you need is to notice what is happening already in your body, small physical signs that you may have previously ignored and then start to recognise whether your feelings are towards the lower end of the scale of arousal. Arousal starts from a low point at which it's perfectly possible to manage your life and responsibilities and still be aware that there are some feelings around. You notice a twinge of sadness there, a clench of irritation here, but nothing that interferes too much.

What happens to us, though, over a matter of days, weeks or years, is that the level of arousal increases. This is why it's also useful to know when your emotional levels are rising. Your sleep may become disturbed; you lose your appetite or find yourself eating compulsively; you realise you're drinking more alcohol than usual. You may begin to snap at others or find yourself getting tearful. We recognise these periods as times when we feel particularly 'stressed' and under pressure. Sometimes a release of mental and physical tension is achieved when we erupt with aggression or collapse and succumb to illness or even breakdown.

It is possible to manage this process less dramatically by

releasing emotion harmlessly and privately. Fear can be released through shaking and trembling. Anger can be released through sound – shouting, screaming, singing – and movement – hitting cushions, running, vigorous housework, playing squash. Sadness and grief can be released through tears and sobbing. We are born with this capacity for release, of course, but instead of learning that we must control ourselves at times and still give ourselves permission for release in private, we put a lid on *all* our feelings and their release for an entire lifetime.

When we contain and control our feelings for too long and refuse to explore them, we risk getting into a state where our emotions take over. These can spill over into all parts of our lives but, in the context of this book, remember that when you want to talk about something important, the nearer the high end of the emotional scale you climb, the more difficult it's going to be to stay clear-headed.

So a golden rule for effective communication is to make sure you don't speak up when your levels of emotional arousal are high. It's not fair on yourself because you're too vulnerable, and it's not fair on the other person because of the likelihood that you'll explode, attack or otherwise lose control. So if you are fuming or in floods of tears or in a state of fear or shock . . . *wait*. Put off speaking until you have some emotional distance and have cooled down sufficiently. It may only take an hour; it may take very much longer.

There is a possibility that once you've calmed down, you will rationalise away the whole situation, persuading yourself that you don't really need to tackle it after all! This is a fundamental mistake: on one hand we build up the emotional leverage to give us the momentum to say something we've long wanted to say and on the other, from a cooler distance, we then minimise our complaint into non-existence.

This approach with its three essential questions helps you include the emotion to strengthen your communication, but without letting it reach levels where it will only mess up the whole interaction. This is enough to begin to take responsibility for your feelings. Getting accustomed to your own emotional landscape – its irregularities, its sensitivities, the danger signs, your emotional needs and rhythms – can help towards long-term emotional management. For now, though, it is enough to recognise your own emotional clues with curiosity and without censure. This will help you find the truthful answer to the question 'How do I feel?'

Question Three: What do you want to be different?

This final question is even more of a challenge. Even if you get as far as anwering the first two questions, it is this one that will be the acid test: it will transform a mere complaint (what you do and how I feel about it) into a constructive comment or request. When anyone asks how you make criticism constructive, this is the answer: you suggest what you would like to be different. Not as an order or a nag or a threat or a vague hint but spelt out as a clear alternative. You may not get what you want but the only way you'll ever find out is by stating it clearly.

This needn't be complicated. Sometimes it is enough to state 'I'd like you to stop'. This is clear and to the point should you object to someone using language that you find offensive or to an individual who, without invitation, insists on stroking your arm while talking to you.

Most answers, after a little consideration, are straightforward

● I'd like you to stop shouting at me

- I'd prefer you to consult me before making an arrangement

- I'd like you to check everything that leaves the office

Why do we need to know what we want?

The reason for the answer to the question 'What do you want to be different?' is a measure of this process as an exchange rather than indiscriminate attack. If we want to confront directly but without aggression, which is what causes the damage, then we have to stop focusing exclusively on status and rank and other external factors. We have to look at the whole, through equal eyes. This means remembering you have as much right to speak as the next person and that it is possible, if you are specific, to engage in a reciprocal discussion instead of a battle.

Suddenly, then, this confrontation ceases to be a question of ME telling YOU where to get off because YOU basically have no right to behave like that because MY wants and needs matter more! This roughly encapsulates the main features of our usual and familiar pattern: effective in the short term possibly but, as in Antonia's situation with her au pair, not advantageous in terms of your relationships with others in the longer term.

Here is the paradigm for answering the third question: Taking a step back, you start to see the process as ME informing YOU that I have a problem with this aspect of YOUR behaviour. I feel (fill in blank) about it and I would prefer you to do this (fill in blank). Do you agree/understand? Is this possible? Can we work something out together?

Most people are surprised by the need to clarify this third answer. You may protest that it sounds too trivial and really shouldn't need to be said. This may be so in a fantasy world where everyone can successfully intuit (and meet) our innermost needs, but, in our current world, it certainly helps the other person to know precisely what it is you do want. The most constructive gesture you can make, whenever you are being in any way critical, is to spell out exactly what you want of the other person and how this would improve on what is currently happening.

There are two of you involved

This third question creates a situation where it is possible for you to open a genuinely reciprocal dialogue. Without this, all you'll achieve is the delivery of a criticism. You could argue that this is the point. All you want to do is criticise, so why not simply state the criticism without bothering with all of this? Without this two-way dialogue, though, simply communicating the answers to the first two questions alone will have an aggressive effect. Yes, the other person will get a clear message. Depending on the power dynamic at the time – parent to child/junior to senior – the person on the receiving end will respond with protest or deference. You may get the desired change you want, but the inequality – experienced as injustice or indignity – will never be forgotten. This is how the seeds of resentment are sown and how you unwittingly cause the very defensiveness you are seeking to avoid.

The aim of this whole process is obviously to communicate about a difficult issue without the whole thing degenerating into aggression. Since assertive communication is reciprocal, i.e. it is *between* two people rather than a dictate from one on high to one lower down, we have to *consider the other person as well*. This means that you establish a situation in which the other person has a voice as well: the other person is also empowered to have their say on an issue and, most importantly, has a choice of response.

Think of the negativity surrounding the prospect of criticism. We don't like it at all. None of us welcomes criticism because past experience means we often carry feelings of hurt and bitterness towards particular people for their criticisms of us, especially the unfair ones that left us feeling powerless to retaliate at the time. So it's understandable that when someone gets a whiff of criticism, they defend themselves from anticipated attack. This is so automatic we could call it a knee-jerk response to criticism.

Even if you're simply trying to talk about a difficult issue, it is quite possible that the other person will imagine they're being criticised and will still respond defensively. We are all sensitive to criticism and extremely sensitive to criticism of certain areas of our lives: our abilities as parents, lovers, drivers; our professional competence or appearance. We have individual 'sore spots', but our initial response to criticism is usually one of vulnerability and therefore defensiveness.

Our sensitivity to the potential for harm in criticism acts as a deterrent to speaking up. However, instead of letting your worries hold you back from saying anything at all, you can usefully carry these concerns in your awareness when you approach these issues to help you move forward with care. The answer to this third question – 'What would you like to be different?' – helps you do this in two ways. First, it helps you focus on one specific thing that you want. If you are asking for a specific change in behaviour, this will be received differently from asking someone to be a different kind of *person*. 'I'd like us to find a way of spending more time on our own together' is different from 'I wish you weren't so busy': 'I'd like you to come in at 9 a.m.' is more helpful than 'You've got to learn to be more punctual'.

Watch out for the habit of wishing people – lovers, children, managers, employees, friends, parents – were more the kind of people you have in mind for them to be! How can anyone respond to this kind of request without feeling overwhelmed and impotent? How can they possibly agree or hope to match up to your ideals? Inevitably and understandably, overt or covert hostility will emerge in response.

Most of us will respond positively to being asked to change something that is within our capability of changing. We may not like it but if the request is reasonable and clearly stated without being an attack, most of us respond with co-operation. All you can do, therefore, if you want to criticise someone, is to bear in mind that your best chance is to have thought through your answer *before* you start speaking. It doesn't guarantee you'll get what you're asking for but it will put you in the best position for negotiation.

This third question is very confronting. It challenges you to be truthful about whether you simply want to let rip at someone and have a good moan, or whether you are genuinely interested in an equal interaction. This presents you with a choice.

... provides you with a choice

Am I going to confront this? Do I really want to find a way forward? Or do I simply want to build up a few prime grievances so that I can feel sorry for myself? Do I prefer to feel superior to others or stay convinced that I'm a hapless victim of those around me? Or am I going to speak up? The choice is yours.

If you have answers to all three questions, you can now move forward to put them into practice.

Chapter Seven

Putting perpendicular and personal power together

As we've seen, we don't always have a choice as to our position on the ladder of perpendicular power. We find ourselves with this power through circumstances beyond our control, or as part and parcel of our roles and responsibilities. It's important not to split the two kinds of power into bad and good simply because perpendicular power in our world so easily fosters exploitation, abuse and oppression. Having power over others through expertise or resources, possessing status and being higher up the ladder of authority offer us a choice: do we wield this power as a weapon or handle it with care and responsibility? What prevents perpendicular power becoming oppressive is when we balance it with the principles of personal power.

How would it affect both the interactions we looked at earlier if Antonia and Maggie (see pages 12–16) had taken a different approach? In both instances, perpendicular power was then the only reference.

Antonia and Ingrid

When Antonia gave her au pair, Ingrid, a legitimate criticism, one of the pitfalls was her lack of a clear request. She complained about what was wrong but didn't ever come up with her third answer, assuming, as we do, that it was obvious.

Like many who are accustomed to offering criticism in this way, Antonia probably didn't give it another thought. Often, when we believe we have no difficulty with confronting others, it is precisely because this is the manner in which we do it: reinforcing our status to make sure we get a 'result'. The consequences of correcting someone's behaviour under coercion or through intimidation means that equality never comes into it. There is no choice, no chance of co-operation, no chance for anything remotely creative.

Whenever we correct someone in this way, the process (like Antonia's) often reveals:

- No specific request, only a complaint

- The tendency to pile on the blows while we've got the upper hand and then

- The final blow: to reprimand them for having the audacity to show a response to your treatment, 'Don't you get angry with me' and so on

So what difference would it make if Antonia were to confront Ingrid with an approach that balanced *both* kinds of power?

For a start she'd have to answer her three questions.

Q: What is happening?

A: The children weren't ready for bed

Q: How do you feel?

A: I feel annoyed

Q: What would you like to be different?

A: I'd like Ingrid to make sure they are ready by the time I get home around 7 o'clock.

Imagine a new scene at breakfast time in the kitchen

Antonia: 'Ingrid, I'd like a quick word with you.'

Ingrid: 'Sure. What is it?'

Antonia: 'I was annoyed last night when I got home and found the children still not ready for bed. I'd really like you to make sure they are. It's important to me.'

Ingrid: 'I'm so sorry. I took them to the park and I forgot the time.'

Antonia: 'OK. Well, can you make sure you come back earlier so you can get them ready for bed by 7?'

Ingrid nods: 'Of course, I'm sorry.'

Antonia: 'Don't worry. I'm glad we've been able to talk about it.'

(Time to close.)

Antonia: 'I've got to fly.' (Goes to kiss goodbye to the children.)

Antonia will still get what she wants, but this time she leaves behind her a wholly different experience, without the slightest trace of aggression. Ingrid may still feel reprimanded but the manner in which the criticism was given is unlikely to leave her feeling defensive or resentful: her behaviour was corrected as an employee but she wasn't personally attacked. This is how the two kinds of power work together in balance.

Whenever you want to correct someone, you'll find it more straightforward when you're dealing, like Antonia, with a one-off occurrence. It is also more manageable when we deal with a problem soon after it happens. Actually doing this, however, is rare. Most of us, most of the time do not respond to individual incidents but keep quiet, for a multitude of reasons. This leads to an accumulation of pebbles – each pebble representing a single incident we failed to deal with – and over the course of time, we often find we have accumulated a dauntingly large pile.

This makes the problem harder to deal with because our unexpressed feelings also accumulate. What might once have been a straightforward issue becomes muddled and clouded by anger, helplessness or both. It all seems too much now and we resign ourselves to 'the way things are' or we grab one pebble from somewhere in the pile to chuck at someone, only to find that several other pebbles become dislodged in the process, and we end up piling on as many criticisms as we have to hand.

This doesn't mean that we can't approach a situation in our lives that has built up a 'history', but it does mean we need to go carefully. In these instances, it is useful to regard your opening statement as a preamble to a genuinely reciprocal discussion about the situation between you both, a way of opening a door that has been closed. So your third answer becomes 'I'd like us to be able to talk about this and find out where we go from here'. This takes into account that the other person may also have feelings about the situation that you will need to listen to as well.

The implication is that putting aside whoever has done what

in the past, this is currently the situation and that you both need to take equal responsibility for sorting it out. This is where equality comes in. The manner in which you make this overture is crucial: even a small hint of aggression or blame will provoke the other person to shut down in self-defence. When taking this kind of initiative, aim for an invitation rather than a threat.

The manner in which you suggest to someone that you sit down and talk needs to indicate an openness to work something out together. It is an ideal approach when a conflict of needs or wills presents us with the necessity to find a compromise co-operatively. It's still essential to have considered and answered your three key questions beforehand. You need to have in mind your third answer, even if you are then going to initiate a discussion, as in the following illustration.

Maggie and Rick

Maggie was left feeling helpless about the stalemate between herself and Rick, her teenaged son: she nags because he won't listen and he won't listen because she nags. When you want to tackle a pile of grievances like this, you have to make a choice: do I want to pick over the pile or do I want to move on? You go back or you go forward. You cannot do *both*.

Maggie decides she wants to move on. She decides she'll approach Rick at a neutral time on Saturday morning when neither is rushing off somewhere. They are both in the kitchen. Rick is having breakfast.

> *Maggie: (sitting down at the table to join him) 'Rick, there's something I want to talk about.'*

> Rick (visibly bristling): 'For Christ's sake, Mum, *don't* start.'

> *Maggie: 'I know, Rick, I've got it wrong in the past but this is*

very difficult for me. I want you to hear me out. Please.'

Rick looks at her, saying nothing.

Maggie takes a deep breath and continues: 'I've been think-ing about this a lot and I want to sort something out. It really drives me mad that you won't help with stuff around the house but what makes it worse is that I'm still playing moth-er. You're not a child any more and I don't want to nag you. I hate it and you hate it. So I want us to find a way to com-municate differently (specific request).'

Rick (a bit puzzled but not defensive): 'What do you mean?'

Maggie: 'I'm not sure what I mean. I don't have a plan. I just want us to sit down and talk because I want you to help. I don't want to have to keep chasing you: I'm tired of doing that. I want you to take some responsibility for helping. Will you think about it and then let me know what you're pre-pared to do and when?'

Rick (playing dumb): 'What am I meant to be thinking about?'

Maggie: 'I want you to come up with a constructive sugges-tion as to how you can do your share of the work around the house.'

Rick (sighs): 'OK. I'll think about it.'

Maggie: 'Good. Have a think and then we can talk again. How about tomorrow evening?'

Rick: 'I'm playing squash tomorrow.'

Maggie: 'When do you have to leave?'

Rick: 'Seven.'

Maggie: *'In that case, let's talk at 6.30 so we've got time before you go. I want us to find a solution.'*

Rick: 'All right, Mum, I got the message!'

(Time to close.)

Maggie gets up and walks out of the kitchen.

This is an illustration of how to leave the pile behind and move forward. What Maggie does well here is strike a balance between keeping it focused yet informal at the same time. Making sure they can talk again at a specific time is crucial: without this she won't know when to bring up the subject again.

The structure I am suggesting here gives *boundaries* to the interaction. This is because we cannot pretend that this is a normal conversation like any other. We can be spontaneous and unselfconscious 90 per cent of the time but these situations in our lives, because we have so much invested in them, and because there is often so much past entanglement, are *different*. We need to handle them in a special way. We need boundaries because if we don't limit what we say, it's almost a guarantee that everything will get out of hand.

Making a structure like this will feel very odd at first. You'll feel self-conscious because this is not how you would 'normally' speak or behave. You wouldn't normally make a date to speak to your own son or approach a friend in a formal manner. But given the delicacy of the topic, which is precisely why you have to tread carefully, there is no point in pretending otherwise. What you should find is that even if the other party is a little puzzled by this approach, they won't feel the need to defend themselves. This then gives you the best chance of being heard and therefore being able to sort out what's gone wrong between you.

Part 2

The practice

Chapter Eight

Committing theory to practice

Let's look at other examples of everyday scenarios in which our new approach can be applied. Here are three individuals who want to initiate a tricky discussion with someone in their lives whom they don't want to alienate.

1. **Sally** lives with Pete. They've been going out for about four years and living together almost one year. Everything is fine except that, when stressed, Pete has a habit of losing his temper and whatever Sally says or does will immediately provoke an aggressive outburst. She really doesn't like this and wants to ask him to stop shouting at her.

2. After working abroad for a couple of years, **Rebecca** came home two months ago. She is temping, waiting to start a course in six months' time and is living with her mother in the meantime. Basically they get on well. The problem for Rebecca is that her mother has, a couple of times now, made arrangements for a family get-together at the weekend, and assuming Rebecca would want to be included, simply announced it to her when she came in from work.

Rebecca doesn't want this to happen again.

3. **Dawn** runs a busy PR department in a large company. She is generally pleased with her work of her secretary, Emma, but a week ago happened to find a couple of envelopes with an incomplete postcode in the pile waiting to go off in the mail. She is surprised because Emma has always seemed very methodical and she wants to say something because she's now worried that she can't continue to rely on Emma to be careful in the future.

Each of the three individuals has done their 'homework' and come up with answers to their three questions:

- *What is happening?*

- *How do you feel about it?*

- *What would you like to be different?*

▶ SALLY

Pete gets angry and takes it out on me.
I don't like it.
I want him to stop.

Looking at these answers a little more closely, Sally needs to be careful regarding the first answer. This is because criticising someone for being angry risks being inflammatory. People can't help what they feel but they can, of course, help how they *express* their feelings. She'll need to avoid blaming Pete for his feelings because this will only make things worse.

▶ **REBECCA**

My Mum makes arrangements that include me but without consulting me.
I get annoyed.
I want her to stop treating me like a child and treat me like an adult instead.

The problem in this situation is the answer to the third question 'What would you like to be different?'. We often fall into the trap of interpreting someone else's behaviour and presenting it to them as a fact. Why is this potentially explosive? The answer is because interpretation always provides a vehicle for blame and blame is an aspect of aggression that we're trying to avoid. There's a big difference (on the receiving end) to be told 'Stop treating me like a child' and the request 'I'd like you to ask me before making an arrangement'. Rebecca will have to change her third answer to one that is less emotive and more specific if she wants to avoid her request coming across as an accusation.

▶ **DAWN**

My secretary isn't being careful enough.
I'm surprised.
I want her to double-check everything.

The potential difficulty here comes in the second answer. The word 'surprised' in this context often carries an overtone of disappointment which can cause problems. None of us responds well to the implication that we have fallen short of someone else's expectations. Given this particular context, where Dawn is criticising someone junior, she'll have to take care to avoid talking from 'on high', but instead make sure she maintains a view of equality.

Timing

Before we look at the dialogue between each pair, it's essential to consider a further aspect of preparation. If asked when they might consider making their approach, both Sally and Rebecca will, like anyone else, imagine they'll wait until it happens again. Sally will wait for Pete to get angry again before she says something. Rebecca will wait until her mother springs another family outing on her as she's coming in the door. Dawn is likely to wait until an opportune moment presents itself for her to speak to Emma.

We wait in this way because we are anxious and we think that we will handle it better either when it happens next time, or when we can find the right moment. However, waiting until it happens again is *always* a recipe for disaster. Always, always, always. The whole point about these particular issues in our lives is that they are tricky. They have become issues precisely because we are apprehensive about dealing with them for the reasons we've already seen. We're quite right to feel anxious because the situations are full of potential to go wrong. The teaching in this book is how to work *with* that anxiety instead of letting it control and clamp down on our behaviour and communication.

Think of these guidelines as markers to follow through the difficulties. It would be highly improbable that any sensitive human being could tackle these conversations without feeling apprehensive. Instead of seeing your anxiety as negative and a sign of weakness, regard it as a sign of mental health: a notable absence of anxiety on your part is likely to indicate an excess of self-righteousness or vindictiveness, with a corresponding lack of concern for the other person.

Given that you know you'll be anxious, you have to give yourself the best chance possible of communicating from a clear base. You can choose when to speak up. If you wait until the next time, which is what we are all tempted to do, it is virtually impossible to keep your own focus. When Sally is once again having to deal with the actuality of Pete yelling at her, she is not going to think clearly: she'll respond again with frustration and anxiety which won't be effective: she is instinctively going to want to defend herself instead. We need to speak from a place of relative emotional calm, rather than in a state of high agitation or extreme distress.

Timing is also imperative in Rebecca's situation. If she comes home, tired at the end of the day, to be greeted by her mother's cheery announcement that she's arranged a family picnic, what is likely to happen? In the heat of the moment, Rebecca's emotional momentum will be fuelled by all the previous occasions on which her mother has 'treated her like a child', plus the fact that her unexpressed resentment has been building up for a while. The likelihood of Rebecca not lashing out is slim. She will probably end up making accusations and this will lead to exactly the bad feeling between the two of them that she so much wants to avoid.

Dawn's situation illustrates a different kind of waiting. She isn't waiting for it to happen again because she wants to discuss what, she hopes, was a one-off lapse on Emma's part. But she is still waiting for the 'right' moment to present itself! This strategy never helps. The prospect of what Dawn needs to say is going to linger on the edges of every other interaction she has with Emma. She'll wonder whether this is the right time, hoping to tag it on to the end of another conversation or when there's a convenient break between other demands. In this way, Dawn's anxiety will build up in response to the lingering tension of something unspoken between them. What's more, Emma will probably pick up this tension as well, even if she has no idea what it is about.

Personal power is badly affected by the habit of postponement. Of course, waiting sometimes teaches us to be patient and to yield to the forces around us, but waiting can become a chronic pattern of deferment and aggravation. When waiting doesn't increase your equilibrium but, instead, only serves to maintain a constant level of anxiety, consider it unhelpful. Waiting too long and too often to speak up in any situation makes you more dependent on outside factors – being given permission, an invitation, a chance opportunity by someone else – and makes it harder for you to take charge of anxiety and move through it. Hence the next strategy.

Taking the initiative and setting the scene

Instead of waiting, the key is to take the initiative, a move that gives a huge boost to personal power. This means setting the scene: planning in advance a time to speak, making an appointment or setting a specific time aside. It means taking 'time out' from normal interaction, whether at home, at work or in a social setting. This helps in several ways.

If Dawn makes a specific time to talk to Emma, she is interrupting the cycle of wondering and worrying, and will give herself the best opportunity to remain clear and focused. Also, by setting time aside, it makes this interaction special in some way. It marks it as important. This doesn't have to mean it's life shattering, but it matters because it has been bugging her enough to want to sort it out. Given both the cultural constraints about saying anything directly, and the easier options of sniping and swiping, the choice to tackle a situation in this way is always important.

When Rebecca says to her mum that she wants to sit down and talk about something that's bothering her, her mother may well be puzzled by her daughter's approach. However, as you'll see as we go though this process, people can survive a few moments of being puzzled far more easily than an unexpected barrage of accusation.

The idea of setting time aside makes us feel awkward because it seems formal. It is, in fact, a bit formal, but this is in order to safeguard the opportunity to get through this conversation without a battle. So while it's tempting to try and have this conversation while someone's trying to watch TV, or while you're in the middle of having dinner, or just before you're due to go out together, don't! Think about timing.

At work, too, we get so anxious that we take any chance to initiate a serious discussion: bumping into the person in the corridor or catching them after a long meeting. At home and at work, our anxiety undermines our judgement so we choose the wrong moments or the wrong places and then wonder why it doesn't go as we'd planned. This is why taking the initiative is so vital because turning everything on its head, you start *before* the anxiety gets the better of you. You may feel silly, awkward, stupid, clumsy, embarrassed ... that's fine! Starting in this way gives you and the other person a better chance of being able to communicate. As you'll find, setting the scene is the only way to start if you want to get through to the other side without falling foul of each other.

Chapter Nine

Talking it through

Sally and Pete

Setting the scene: Sally decides to talk to Pete when they're sitting at home after dinner. Pete's watching television but nothing especially important.

Sally: *'Pete, I want to talk to you about something.'*

Pete: 'What?'

Sally: *'Just something I've wanted to say.'*

Pete (his eyes still on the screen): 'Well, say it then.'

Sally: *'I need you to listen to me.'*

Pete: 'I am listening.' (Looking at her.) 'What's the matter?'

Sally: *'Nothing's the matter ... well, yes, there is something actually.'* (She takes a breath.) *'Pete, I need us to talk about you shouting at me.'*

Pete: 'I'm not shouting at you.'

Sally: 'No, not now, but you do often when you're worked up about something.'

Pete: 'Everybody does. It's quite normal.' (Beginning to feel slightly defensive.)

Sally senses this: 'I get upset, Pete. I don't think it's fair that you should take things out on me and ...'

Pete: 'I *don't* take things out on you. What are you going on about? I really don't need this hassle right now.' (He gets up and goes into the kitchen.)

Learning

It's easy here to assume that Pete is being an insensitive brute. How can he not see that poor Sally is struggling? We generally find it much easier to assume that someone's reaction is automatically due to some latent boorishness or unpleasantness: it's then possible to overlook completely that this response is exactly that, a response. Let's look at Sally's communication more carefully.

What's gone wrong is due to a common tendency to *under*state our feelings and the importance of what we want to ask for. At the moment, Sally's anxiety is getting the upper hand. This makes her comes across as vague and almost on the verge of whinging. Whinging always gets the other person's back up so is best avoided. How can she improve her communication?

There's more to learn about how you answer the second question: 'How do you feel about what's happening?' Standing on the threshold of opening this kind of dialogue, we feel all sorts of feelings: anxiety, awkwardness, nervousness. The best chance we have of managing these feelings is by putting them into words instead of trying to disguise them, as Sally did, in order to pretend that we are really quite comfortable and laid back about the whole matter when in reality we're not. This kind of pretence is only for show: it's part of the rules of display in any aggressive encounter that you hide any weakness from your opponent so as to gain the upper hand. We do it without thinking. We've mistakenly learned that feelings are weak, that vulnerability is embarrassing, that weakness is bad.

Remember our dread of confrontation generates fear that, when disguised as defensiveness, provokes aggression in the person to whom we're speaking. Time after time after time, this dynamic undermines our best-laid plans and intentions for a meaningful conversation that we really want to have with someone. This is why the honesty intrinsic to this process is so very important.

Putting feelings back into our vocabulary without blame is an immeasurable help to communication, whereas denying them puts you at odds with yourself. If you're anxious, you're anxious: if you feel embarrassed, you feel embarrassed. Once you've put this small reality into words that match the feeling, you can move through it. Feelings need not be a nuisance, interfering with how you would like to be.

Express what you feel and move on through the anxiety to what you find next. Once you get the hang of this, you'll be amazed at how much stronger you'll feel in yourself. This is another vital aspect of personal power. It makes all the difference to the conversation you're going to have. Feelings help to transform a rehearsed script into a dialogue with meaning. It is our feelings that bring the words to life.

It will also help Sally if she is more specific than 'upset'. Avoid the word 'upset' because this is an umbrella term that can mean cross, angry, hurt, worried or frightened in different situations. She needs to be more precise. Here's Practice 2.

▶ PRACTICE 2

Sally: 'Pete, I want us to have a talk about something. It's something that's really important to me and I'm feeling very awkward about bringing it up.'

Pete (his attention on her): 'What on earth's the matter?'

Sally: 'Can we turn the telly off a minute?'

Pete looks surprised but picks up the control and turns it off. He sits back and looks at her.

Sally (with a nervous laugh): 'Oh dear! I'm feeling so nervous. It's ridiculous.'(It isn't really but this is what she feels, so it's better to say it. She takes a deep breath.) 'Pete, what I want to say is that when you shout at me, as you do sometimes when you get too stressed, I really don't like it.'

Pete (looking a little mystified but not defensive): 'When do I shout at you? I'm not aware of shouting at you, not that much anyway. You shouldn't take it personally.'

Sally: 'I do take it personally. It's me you're shouting at. I'm sure you don't know you're doing it and I know deep down that it's not me that you're angry at but ... (it suddenly comes to her) I hate it, Pete, I really hate it. It may sound pathetic but I really get frightened.'

Pete is now a little alarmed: 'Why didn't you say so?'

Sally considers this: 'I don't know. I guess I didn't want to make you worse.'

There is a short silence.

Pete: 'Well, what do you want me to do? Be sweetness and light all the time?'

Sally (this is where the third answer comes in handy): 'No. All I know is I'd like you to stop shouting at me. Maybe there's another way you can deal with things when you get very stressed.'

Pete shrugs his shoulders and sighs: 'I dunno what to say.'

This is a crucial moment in any difficult conversation that you've initiated.

At this point, Sally needs to close. She started it and has to end it. It's not the end of the whole story. They may come back to it. There may be further discussion. But right now, the task Sally set herself is complete. To continue at this point is to risk returning to the emotional minefield once you've successfully navigated a route through it. You feel so relieved sometimes that, on a crest of false euphoria, you are tempted to launch into another thing you've always meant to mention ... with inevitably disastrous consequences.

Closing is necessary for you to keep a boundary about what you wanted to say and to keep within that boundary. It is equally important for the other person. Here, Pete needs time to think. Unlike, Sally, he hasn't spent weeks thinking about this issue. It is all completely new to him so he needs the space to reflect.

Sally: 'We don't need to find an answer now. I'm feeling a lot better now that we've talked.' (She smiles at him.) 'Let's put the telly back on. Do you want a cup of tea or something?' (Gets up to go to the kitchen.)

How will these same principles apply to Rebecca's situation?

Rebecca and Mum

Setting the scene: Rebecca decides to have a talk with her mother when there's time to talk on Saturday morning. They are in the kitchen, Rebecca sitting at the table and her mother is emptying the dishwasher.

Rebecca: 'Mum, I want to talk to you about something.'

Mum (continuing to open cupboards to put stuff away): 'What is it?'

Rebecca: 'I'll wait until you're finished.'

Her mother looks puzzled and then turns round: 'So what is so important? You're worrying me.'

Rebecca: 'It's nothing to worry about. It's just that I've been meaning to say something for a while about, well, it's when you make arrangements, like next weekend going to Chris and Julie's for the barbecue and sometimes I don't always feel like going ...'

Mum: 'What do you mean you don't feel like going? It's only your own family.'

Rebecca: 'I know it's only family but you don't ask me first if I want to go.'

Mum: 'Well, I'm sorry. I didn't know you had other plans. You didn't tell me.'

Rebecca: 'I don't necessarily have other plans. It's just that I feel you're treating me like a child when you don't consult me.'

Mum: 'Well, I thought you'd enjoy seeing everybody. You've been away a long time and I thought you'd like it. What are you going to do instead? Sit around here and mope around?'

Rebecca (exasperated): 'Mum, just stop treating me like this. I'm an adult now. I'm only living here until I can find somewhere of my own ...'(Realising that this sounds hurtful, her voice tails off.)

Learning

Rebecca also has to find a more transparent way of expressing her feelings. These interactions aren't easy – if they were, we'd have little concern and a lot more confidence. As it is, though, we are bound to feel worried about alienating someone close to us or creating bad feeling. Approaching a parent is on the heavyweight list because of the existence of our whole history – a shared history compiled of deep and complex events and reactions – which makes for a huge emotional tangle. We need to tread lightly and keep to the boundaries of the three answers: what will help to maintain an awareness of our feelings.

This is a skill that few of us are taught. But it can be learned. How would it change the interaction between Rebecca and her mother if she were to be clearer about her feelings and not to fall into the habit of blame? Here's Practice 2.

▶ **PRACTICE 2**

Rebecca: 'Mum, there's something I want to talk to you about.

Mum: 'What is it?'

Rebecca: *'Come and sit down a minute. It's something important and I'm feeling anxious about bringing it up because I don't want us to have a row.'*

Mum: *'Why on earth should we?'*

Rebecca: *' Well, there's something on my mind to tell you but it's difficult because I know you're doing it for the best.'* (She pauses.)

Are we ever going to get there?

Mum looks at Rebecca, waiting.

Rebecca takes a breath: *'You really make me cross when you make arrangements, social arrangements, like the barbecue next weekend, for example. I feel you're not treating me like an adult, you know, you don't ask me first.'*

Mum starts getting a little defensive at this point.

Why? Rebecca started well and got going in an effective way but then she made the mistake of saying first 'You make me cross ...' then' ... I feel you're not treating me like an adult.' The first is an accusation, the second is a statement of apparent fact. Both of these phrases are indirectly aggressive and will guarantee a defensive response. Feelings need to describe *feelings*, not opinions or thoughts. Here's Practice 3.

▶ PRACTICE 3

Rebecca: *'Mum, there's something I want to talk to you about. It's important. Can we sit down a minute?'*

Mum: *'What on earth's the matter?'*

Rebecca: 'It's hard for me to bring this up, Mum, because I don't want to have a row. The thing is (she takes a breath) that when you make arrangements for me – things to do at the weekend, you know like the barbecue at Chris and Julie's – I feel really irritated. I don't know what it is but I end up feeling like a child because you've arranged something without asking me. Can you see what I mean?'

Mum: 'Well, I hadn't thought of it like that. I just expected you'd want to see the family so I started organising things. I thought you'd *like* it.'

Rebecca: 'I know, Mum. I'm sure you did. All I'm asking you to do is to check with me first.'

Mum: 'Even if I know you're not doing anything else?'

Rebecca: 'Yes. I'd really appreciate it if you'd check so I can make a choice. Is that OK?'

Mum: 'Yes, I suppose so. I don't understand you sometimes, Rebecca.'

Rebecca smiles.

(Time to close.)

'Right, I'm going to the supermarket. Do you want to come or is there anything we need that you want me to get?'

Simple, honest statements of feeling are an invaluable aid to communication and help to avoid the usual pitfalls.

Dawn and Emma

Finally, we look at Dawn's experience. This is different in that the relationship is confined to the workplace so there is less emotional investment. But it will still be important to express feelings. Dawn is the head of the department and so has legitimate power over Emma. She is not concerned about a row but is more fearful of ill feeling left between them, which would adversely affect their working relationship.

How can she manage her legitimate authority to criticise and ask for a correction in her secretary's work, and at the same time treat her as an equal? She needs to balance her authority over an employee with an equal regard for Emma as a person. This is one of the consequences of using the skill of expressing our feelings.

Setting the scene: Dawn has decided to ask Emma to come into her office to see her. This keeps it separate from other ongoing work together. This is the point of taking 'time out' – to keep the boundary firmly around the actual confrontation.

Dawn: 'Thanks for coming in, Emma. There's something that's been on my mind. A couple of weeks ago, I noticed on your desk some of the mailing for the Patterson project and I saw that the postcodes on some of the envelopes were missing. So I'm wondering if you could make sure it doesn't happen again. It doesn't look good to make that kind of mistake when we're a PR department.'

Emma (a little confused about why she has been called in for this): 'OK. Is that it?'

Learning

Not a bad attempt but a little vague. Dawn needs to be more precise in her request for change. As it stands, she doesn't know if this was a one-off lapse or something more serious. If she wants to be reassured, she needs to be more specific. Here's Practice 2.

▶ **PRACTICE 2**

> *Dawn: 'Thanks for coming in, Emma. I wanted to talk to you about the fact that I happened to notice some of the envelopes you sent out for the Patterson project weren't complete. I was a bit surprised, to be honest, because you're normally very efficient but it's really not acceptable, you know.' (Sits back and smiles sweetly.)*
>
> Emma (feeling confused and criticised but without knowing exactly what it's about): 'What do you mean, they weren't complete?'
>
> *Dawn: 'The postcodes were incomplete. You need to make sure they are complete.'*
>
> Emma: 'OK. Sorry.'
>
> An awkward silence hovers between the two of them.

Learning

When we're nervous, we often lapse into the habit of being authoritarian in tone of voice. This will always generate discomfort in the other person. Dawn needs to express her feelings more clearly.

▶ PRACTICE 3

Dawn: 'Thanks for coming in Emma. I feel a bit awkward about saying this because I'm very pleased with your work. But . . . I happened to see that some of the envelopes in the Patterson mailing were incomplete. They didn't have a postcode. I didn't check them all but it left me very worried. I rely on you to take responsibility for things like that. Do you have any idea what went wrong?'

Emma (somewhat taken aback): 'I hadn't realised. It was just a bit of a rush, that's all.'

Dawn: 'Yes, it was, I know. But it matters a lot to me, you see, because we are a PR department and it's essential that whatever leaves here looks good. I don't want to have to keep checking up on your work so I'd like you to double-check everything in the future. If there's a problem with time, I'd like you to let me know. Can you do that?'

Emma (embarrassed, but aware she is being treated as a member of the team and not like a naughty child): 'Sure. I'm really sorry.'

Dawn: *'It was obviously an oversight. As I said, I'm delighted with your work. I'm glad we've been able to talk about it.'*

(Time to close.)

Dawn stands up, indicating to Emma that the meeting is at an end: 'Thanks for coming. We'd better get back to work. I'll be round later this morning to talk about our meeting tomorrow.'

This is one example of how we can balance a position of authority over someone with the equality of personal power. Dawn manages to criticise a junior with clarity and effectiveness while avoiding aggression.

Chapter Ten

Letting go of the need to blame

We love to blame. Whenever we are unhappy, we find someone or something to blame. When things go wrong, we blame others – or ourselves. When a 'problem' arises in our dealings with people, we resent it, as if its mere appearance accuses us of falling short, of having a less than perfect relationship. A problem always seems to strike us as negative. A key issue, therefore, when considering bringing up a difficult topic is who is to blame. We restrict ourselves to only two alternatives: 'It's your fault' (blame) or 'It's my fault' (guilt). We sift endlessly through misdemeanours and lapses with partners, relations, colleagues and friends, all in order to apportion blame.

When you blame someone else, it's easy to feel a sense of 'righteous' anger that gives you permission to approach them from a superior position. Blaming yourself often means that you keep quiet, because being in the under position implies you have no right to speak. Once you resist the need to deal in guilt or blame, both of which, in the end, are quite useless currencies, you discover other possibilities. Your overall perspective expands and other opportunities open up.

Responsibility

One of these opportunities is the notion of responsibility. Whenever we begin to look at a pattern in a relationship – when something has recurred many times, not simply a one-off event – we bring with us a backlog of grievance and frustration. We convince ourselves that if only the other person were more reasonable, more efficient, more amenable, less touchy, a better manager, then our problems would simply disappear!

From this standpoint, we can blissfully ignore the obvious truth that any interactive pattern takes *two* to construct. So when we look at answering the second question – what do we want to change – and find that we have accumulated more than a few grievances, we know we are looking at changing both a pattern in someone's behaviour as well as the pattern of our own response.

This means acknowledging responsibility for our part in what has happened. At this point, we often want to claim victimisation or helplessness but, unless you are a child, and therefore genuinely powerless, you do have a choice. This choice may have been restricted by lack of knowledge of alternative strategies or fear of reprisals but, as adults, we can choose.

So when we adapt to someone else's behaviour by keeping quiet or hedging around certain topics; when we evolve a pattern of deference and compliance in response to someone's behaviour; when we *could* speak up and risk the consequences of being more honest but don't, we are making choices. When we behave in these ways, we give away our personal power. Remember, personal power is centred on integrity and equality. This means setting limits when we need to and balancing care for others with care for ourselves. Balance sounds easy in principle but can be very hard to achieve. As we begin to reflect more honestly on the problematic relationships in our lives, we often uncover a past tendency towards half-hearted compromises. In other words, we go along with things for a quiet life, instead of clearly stating our own needs and taking the trouble to negotiate an agreement on equal terms. We hold back from being completely honest with ourselves for too long only to find we've arrived at a painful point of reckoning.

Commitment to equality demands that we are open to negotiation; but each of us knows that the allowances we make, the excuses with which we console ourselves and the lengths to which we go to avoid 'trouble' are not truthfully a compromise but more a repression of our feelings. Self deception easily ends up as unforgiving intolerance. In other words, when you swallow back too many grievances, you end up with a whole pile of blame that you then feel compelled to dish out.

So, when practising these skills of confrontation, and they

... a repression of our feelings

are skills that have to be learned, it is helpful to consider this matter of your own responsibility for the situation as it now stands. Fifty/fifty. Once you have genuinely acknowledged this, you can proceed to confront and criticise more clearly: without punishment or blame.

Rosie and Ian

Rosie is living with her partner, Ian. She is divorced and has three children from her previous marriage. Her difficulty is that she can't seem to talk about her past with Ian. She finds that whenever she mentions her first husband or refers to things that happened in the past, he flares up and seems to take offence. She hates the tension that seems to hang around for ages afterwards and has tried to keep the peace by avoiding any mention of these topics. In recent weeks, her daughter has been going through difficulties and has been in touch more than usual. Rosie is currently more keenly aware of the problem and the consequent tension with Ian, because every day she is having to deal with matters that involve her past but still feels unable to mention them.

Her answers to the three questions are:

- Ian blows up whenever I mention the past

- I feel frustrated

- I would like to be able to talk about the past without having a row

Setting the scene: Rosie decides to speak to Ian at a moment when they have some time to themselves.

Rosie: 'Ian, there's something we need to talk about.'

Ian looks at Rosie and shrugs his shoulders, as if to say carry on.

Rosie (clears her throat): 'Well, you know Cathy's in a bit of trouble at the moment and I need to be there for her, well, I want to be there for her and I feel that you seem to resent this.'

Ian: 'I don't resent your children. What are you talking about?'

Rosie: 'Well, you don't like me talking about my past.'

Ian: 'I couldn't give a damn if you talk about your past. It's nothing to do with me.'

Rosie: 'That's not true, Ian. You always get irritated as if you're insecure in some way that I really don't understand...'

Ian: 'For God's sake, keep your psychology out of it.' (Turns away to indicate an end to the conversation.)

Learning

This is a tricky situation because Rosie is anxious about having another row. Once again, Ian's response of aggression appears to have come 'out of the blue' ... but it hasn't. Rosie's anxiety – unexpressed – has made it hard for her to avoid the subtle 'up/down' trap that she has fallen into with that little dig about Ian's insecurity. This indirect criticism communicates to Ian that he is behaving unreasonably (according to Rosie's own 'infallible' point of view). Whenever we speak from this moral high ground, however pleasantly, it will always come across as superior and patronising. When patronised or treated as inferior, we get defensive: defensiveness generates aggression and closes the door on communication. This sequence happens over and over again and accounts for the majority of discussions that degenerate into rows.

How can Rosie avoid this and keep the door open? By expressing her nervousness more honestly. Once she comes down from the moral high ground and treats Ian as an equal, she will communicate more clearly. Here's Practice 2.

▶ **Practice 2**

Rosie: 'Ian, there's something I want to talk to you about and I'm feeling really anxious about bringing it up.'

Ian (puzzled) looks at her and waits.

Rosie: 'Basically . . . ' she pauses 'This is really hard. When we talk about my past or when I refer to it, you seem to get defensive. I don't know why . . . '

Ian frowns: 'What do you mean defensive?'

Rosie: 'I don't know, Ian,' (steadily looking at him) 'but whenever I mention my past you don't like it. Surely you've noticed that yourself?'

Ian: 'Your past is nothing to do with me.'

Rosie: 'I know it was all before we met but since we're together now, your past and my past are part of our relationship. I get so frustrated when I can't mention these things.'

Ian: 'Who said you couldn't mention them?'

Rosie: 'Well, you haven't said so exactly but you get so upset that I have stopped saying things. I avoid things because I don't know if you're going to get cross . . . ' (getting into her stride now) ' ... and that's what I don't like, Ian. I don't like having to avoid my past because my children are still around and like Cathy, at the moment, I want to be there for her as well as be with you.'

Ian: 'I don't *make* you avoid your past.'

(Pivotal point in this interaction: blame or responsibility?)

Rosie pauses and then agrees with him: 'No ... you don't. You don't make me avoid it. It's my way of dealing with this situation and I don't want to do it any more. I want to be able to talk about my children and have that be OK.'

Ian doesn't say anything.

Rosie: 'Ian, will you agree to that?'

Ian: 'Sure, I didn't know you found it so difficult.' (Sighs.)

(Time to close now.)

Rosie: 'Thanks for listening.' (Gets up.) 'I'm going to start supper. Do you want anything?'

This interaction illustrates an important point: it was essential that Rosie acknowledged responsibility for her response to Ian's irritation. He quite rightly challenged her when he said he didn't make her keep quiet. She had chosen to keep quiet as her pattern of response to his aggression. In doing this, she had been handing him her personal power. You don't have to immediately make it your 'fault' either: acknowledging *your* part in a pattern is all that's needed to avoid recrimination. Like Maggie, who didn't want to keep chasing after her son, Rosie can see that if she chooses to adapt her own behaviour in a certain way – in this instance with self-imposed censorship – she can also choose to *stop*.

Another aspect of taking responsibility occurs when you fail to express just how much you object to someone's behaviour. You may mention it or joke about it, but when the behaviour doesn't change, you get frustrated. In reviewing the situation, you have to see that the reason the other person often doesn't take on board your irritation is precisely because you don't express it adequately!

Martin and Karen

Martin and Karen have been living together for three years. They get on fine together and plan to get married but Martin has a problem with Karen's punctuality. He likes to be on time for things, whereas she has a tendency to dawdle, dither and rush around at the last minute, doing completely 'unnecessary' chores with the result that they always leave late. He waits and mutters and then becomes short and abrupt with her. She tells him not to be moody and complains she can't change the habit of a lifetime. This means that they set off wherever they're going with a lot of tension between them.

When two people exhibit conflicting patterns of behaviour, it is of course possible that they can rub along together without much bother. We can and do accommodate each other's idiosyncrasies. However, problems occur when one or other of the partners adapts by accommodating the other *beyond* their own limits: in other words, when we suppress our irritation. We rationalise our irritation by telling ourselves it's only minor and it doesn't really matter.

You know it does matter if the irritation grows into a pebble of annoyance. You have to be honest with yourself on these issues. Nobody can sort it out for you. Only you truthfully know whether you are genuinely happy to go along with someone else's behaviour or whether you are denying what you are truly feeling. Denial is always bad news for personal power and if you let it simmer long enough, it will emerge as destructive energy.

Whenever we want to express irritation with a pattern of behaviour that is different from our own, it can easily become a struggle to establish who is right and who is wrong. We believe we need the ballast of superiority to give weight to our cause.

If you can give up the idea of winning and see this interaction somewhat differently – from a place of personal power – you should then see an opportunity to negotiate openly. This means finding a compromise between the two of you. However, if you want to negotiate, you have to fully express your own needs and feelings first, instead of expecting others to grasp the extent of your misery through some magical empathic faculty. There is a good chance that your complaint will be considered seriously if you yourself take your feelings seriously enough to risk direct and honest communication.

Martin has thought through his three answers:

- Karen always leaves getting ready to the last minute

- I get pissed off

- I'd like her to be more punctual

Setting the scene: He decides to approach her, *not* as they are getting ready to go out (!), but when they both have some time one evening to talk, without any pressure.

Martin: 'Can we talk about something?'

Karen (surprised at his question): 'Sure.'

Martin: *'You know when we're getting ready to go out some-where, and I get mad because you're always late ... well, I was wondering if you could make more effort to be on time.'*

Karen: 'I *do* make an effort. I always make an effort.'

Martin: *'But we always leave half an hour late at least . . . for everything.'*

Karen: 'Look Martin, I know you're different. I know you like to get everywhere on the dot but I'm just not like that and I can't change. It's just me, I'm afraid.'

Martin shuts up with a sigh and withdraws.

Martin is finding it difficult to express his feelings fully, but this is the only way he is going to get his message across to Karen without being domineering or bullying. This is what happens when we only have perpendicular power as a reference point. Being more forceful then means exerting more power over the other person. This is when we push, pressurise, threaten, attempt in some way to impose *our* way of thinking, *our* way of seeing, *our* way of behaving on to the other person. Obviously this is aggressive.

Conveying a more powerful message in terms of personal power means keeping away aggression but raising the risk level. It means Martin having the guts to state exactly where he stands on this issue. As long as you keep your cards close to your chest, nobody can get to you, but if you openly say 'This is important and this is what I would like', then you stand without the reins of control to protect you. Instead of controlling the other person, through trying to enforce the outcome of the interaction, you stand there honestly and equally. This takes courage, but it works.

Why does Martin need to express himself more forcefully? Because even if Karen is aware he is irritated by her lack of punctuality, she cannot realise or understand the extent of his irritation. She won't ... unless he tells her.

▶ **PRACTICE 2**

Martin: 'Can we talk about something?'

Karen: 'Sure.'

Martin (pauses): 'Look, Karen, this is really hard for me but I want you to know ... '

Karen (looking at him in alarm): 'What's the matter?'

Martin can't help but smile seeing her anxious face: 'No, it's OK. It's nothing like that. It's about you and I and leaving on time, you know ... '

Karen relaxes: 'Oh that's all ... '

Martin (supersensitive): 'You see, you just dismiss it.'

Karen: 'We've been through all this before.'

Martin: 'I know we've been through this before but I've never told you how I feel. I mean, I know it sounds quirky but it really matters to me not to have to leave in a rush. I hate waiting for you. I get really uptight and it ruins the night out. I don't know why it is but ... I know you're different from me and I can't make you change. But isn't there any way you could take this into account instead of just dismissing it?'

Karen (looking at Martin more thoughtfully now): 'If it bothers you that much, I'll try. I can't promise miracles but I *will* make an effort. OK?' (She leans forward and touches his arm) 'I don't want you to go out feeling uptight. It's not fun for me either.'

(Time to close now.)

Martin sits back and slumps in his chair: 'Well, I'm glad that's over with!'

Karen laughs: 'Was it really that bad?'

Martin: 'Yes, it was! I need to go out for some air to recover! I'll see you later.'

Karen shakes her head, smiling. Martin leaves and goes out.

Closure

You'll notice by now that there is always an emphasis on closing the conversation. You may imagine that this is somewhat artificial: why don't you simply wait until it winds down naturally? Isn't it all going to sound stilted?

The reason for a closure, as with initiating the discussion, is that these are high anxiety times. The mistake we often make is to *pretend* to appear casual. We disguise our nervousness because we think we'll come across more effectively and have a better chance of controlling the outcome of the anticipated dialogue. This is why I lay so much stress on the need to set the scene beforehand, choosing a time and place that is neutral enough to afford both parties the best chances of a successful outcome.

Similarly, when you have said what you need to say and it has been heard, you need to close the door that you've opened. You cannot expect the other person to take responsibility for this: you started it, so you must finish it. This sets firm boundaries around the conversation.

Remember that both parties concerned need a definite closure. These are delicate issues for all of us and prolonged exposure does none of us any good. Closing an interaction is a necessary discipline to acquire. If you don't, then there are many traps lying in store. It is a dangerous time emotionally because you feel exposed. The anxiety we are left with as this kind of dialogue draws to an end stems from fear of some kind of rejection.

All those little gremlins that were chattering in our ears, trying to put us off saying anything beforehand, now resume their task: Is she really going to still want to be friends? What's he going to tell the others? Is he now going to label me as a trouble maker? Was I right to make a fuss? Maybe I should just have kept quiet?

This is why you have to learn to make an exit before these anxieties lead you into dangerous territory. If you don't close definitively you can find yourself going over everything again, conducting a post mortem or, even worse, bringing up a few more 'pebbles' from your collection while you have a captive audience. When anxiety takes over completely, you can even find yourself regretting your earlier clarity and resolve, and end up apologising and possibly retracting your comments!

So be warned. However artificial it feels, learn the discipline of closure. It is equally important for the other person. He or she has travelled over sensitive ground as well as you. More than that, unlike yourself, the other person has not been anticipating the dialogue. What you say often comes as a surprise, especially when it's something you've never mentioned before. So they need time to reflect, consider and digest what you've said.

This whole process demands clarity, decisiveness and firm boundaries. It is a powerful process and if we want to ensure the best possible chance of a constructive outcome, we have to honour those boundaries for all concerned.

Chapter Eleven

Giving due notice

I was recently on a fairly crowded train trying to use the 90-minute journey time to catch up on some reading. Two seats behind me sat a young woman speaking to a friend on her mobile phone. This is often an irritant but her voice was especially penetrating so it aggravated the habit of most mobile phone users, which is to speak at a volume they might use if they were carrying on a conversation across a football pitch.

She regaled her friend with a tale of woe: her parents had refused to drive her to the main station so she had had trouble making her own way to get this particular train. After the relief of a ten minute pause, she then repeated her tale of woe to another friend. Again a pause and then a third repetition.

Her behaviour provoked a lot of response, but none of it direct. The muttered asides from extremely irritated fellow passengers were quite amusing. 'I'm on the train to London,' said the young woman. 'So are we ... !!' several groaned. 'They just left me there sitting on my rucksack ... ' she complained. 'I don't blame them,' went the chorus and so on. What struck me is that throughout these moans and groans and mutterings, this young woman seemed entirely oblivious. She was so pre-occupied with her own misfortunes that she genuinely didn't appear to notice the level of irritation around her. I don't think this was because she was singularly obtuse: it was because nothing was said clearly or directly to her.

This is true for the majority of people. They don't pick up innuendoes, hints, gestures or whispers. Even the very sensitive among us, and I include myself in this category, can be quite surprised by a criticism when it's actually presented. Why? Because without clear, direct communication, it's often impossible to know.

This is why, when you take responsibility for changing a pattern of interaction between you and someone else, you have to consider *when* you do this. If you have willingly or unwillingly set up a system that depends on you continuing to behave in the way you always have done, it makes it especially hard to change. One of our understandable worries is letting the other

... hints, gestures or whispers

person down. If someone has come to depend on us, how can we alter this without causing problems?

Hilary and Jane

Hilary and Jane both attend a yoga class on Thursday evenings. When it emerged during the first class that they lived quite near to one another, Hilary offered to give Jane a lift home. Hilary has let this develop into a pattern because she's trapped in an ongoing routine. Inevitably she is now resentful because all those individual Thursday evening lifts now add up to a grudge directed towards Jane for not realising that it isn't always convenient for Hilary to give her a lift. This particular grudge is well seasoned by a generous dose of that familiar complaint of feeling 'taken for granted'.

Of course, it's easier to 'blame' Jane for lacking sensitivity and not checking out on each occasion whether this was acceptable. She did ask the first few times and guess what? Hilary said it was fine. So Jane stopped asking as Hilary seemed perfectly amenable and never once indicated her true feelings. When the other person takes it on trust that you are offering something genuinely, blaming them for not being sufficiently intuitive to penetrate the layers of pretence is an abdication of your responsibility to be clear.

If Hilary now wants to challenge this pattern directly, she needs to take some responsibility. This is a good example of how we can choose to consider the other person as a pain and a nuisance or acknowledge that it is entirely *in*appropriate to blame someone else for our own lack of clear communication.

Hilary's answers to her three questions are:

● Jane expects a lift home every Thursday

- I resent this

- I'd like her to make her own way home

The third answer has to be thought through very carefully. Does she want to give Jane a lift sometimes or never again? She has to be clear before embarking on this dialogue. We often get ourselves stranded in situations of our own making. We don't exercise our own choice but drift so far along with what we think is expected of us that we end up feeling out of control. So what does Hilary want to be different? After reflection, she decides she doesn't want to say never to Jane, but she'd like not to feel obliged.

How can Hilary take charge of this without laying the blame at Jane's feet? The timing will be crucial. Waiting until the end of the yoga class to announce this to Jane will have an aggressive impact, even if Hilary goes through this whole process step by step. Why? Because by leaving it too late for Jane to make alternative arrangements, she will be denying Jane any options of her own.

This is one of the ways in which we oppress others: by not giving them a clear choice. This 'hit and run' approach is considered normal practice in most institutions and organisations. In our anxiety to avoid confrontation and the possibility of emotional fallout, we confront in a way and at a time when the other person has no opportunity to consider, to agree, disagree or to express their feelings in response to our action.

Should you want to tackle this kind of situation and avoid indirect aggression, you have to give due notice of your intended change of pattern. If you want to make this an equal interaction, based in personal power, then you need to consider the timing. In this instance, Hilary needs to inform Jane in time for her to make other arrangements.

Setting the scene: She has a list of class participants' phone numbers so decides to ring Jane a few days beforehand.

Hilary: 'Hello, Jane. It's Hilary.'

Jane: 'Hilary! What a surprise!'

Hilary: 'Yes. Look, I'm ringing because I'm not going to be able to take you home next Thursday. I'm meeting some friends after the class ...'

Jane: 'That's fine. It's very good of you to take the trouble to let me know. Thank you.'

Hilary: 'OK. Well, see you Thursday then.'

Jane: 'Yes. Bye.'

Hilary has achieved a change in the pattern but has still not confronted it. Jane is likely to assume that this coming Thursday is an exception to the rule. Hilary needs to open up more if she is to do what she really wants to do, which is to interrupt the whole routine. Here's Practice 2:

▶ PRACTICE 2

Hilary: 'Hello, Jane. It's Hilary from the yoga class.'

Jane: 'What a surprise!'

Hilary (clears her throat and takes a breath): 'Jane, look there's something I want to talk about, which isn't easy ... sometimes it's not really convenient to give you a lift home. I wonder if you could get home yourself, you know, sometimes.'

Jane (feeling uncomfortable): 'Well, of course I can ...'

Hilary: 'It's just that it's not always convenient for me.'

Jane (irritated by Hilary's vagueness): 'Well, it sounds as if we'd better leave it, and I'll make my own arrangements OK?'

Hilary: 'Well ... '

Jane: 'That's fine. Bye.'

Hilary is still leaving the effort to Jane. She has to be absolutely clear what she wants to be different: in other words, she must have her third answer in mind before she starts.

▶ PRACTICE 3

Hilary: 'Hello, Jane. It's Hilary from the yoga class.'

Jane: 'Hilary! This is a surprise.'

Hilary: 'Jane, I feel very awkward about this but I haven't been clear in the past and we've got into a routine of travelling back together on Thursdays which isn't always convenient to be honest.'

Jane: 'So should we leave it then?'

Hilary: 'Well, would you mind if, in the future, we checked at the beginning of the class to see what our plans are? Would that be OK?'

Jane: 'Of course it would.'

Hilary: 'I'd really appreciate it if we could do that. I don't want to leave you in the lurch but sometimes I need to make other plans.'

Jane: 'You don't have to keep giving me a lift, you know. If it's easier we can just stop.'

Hilary: 'No, I'd be really happy to still give you a lift sometimes, honestly, but I'd like us to take it one evening at a time. Is that OK?'

Jane: 'That's fine. Thanks for ringing. See you Thursday then.'

Hilary: 'Yes. Bye.'

Finally Hilary takes responsibility, both for reluctantly getting into this routine and then taking the initiative to change it. The whole dialogue is therefore free of blame. It may leave some awkwardness and Jane will probably be more alert to the need to make independent arrangements in the future. Depending on the actual relationship, you could go one stage further.

One of our fears about speaking up is 'How can I say something *after all this time?'*. There is no avoiding the fact that what you say can come as a shock to someone else who has happily gone along with everything, thinking all was fine. From personal experience I know that discovering belatedly the 'truth' of someone's real feelings prompts a mixture of bewilderment, anger and hurt. I'm left with the question: why didn't they think enough of me to treat me as an equal and be *honest*?

Knowing it's going to come as a surprise isn't reason enough to avoid honesty altogether, but it will help if you, as the speaker, can acknowledge this. You don't have to subject someone to an on the spot 'counselling' session, but even in this instance, where Hilary and Jane are not friends, Hilary could add something extra to the dialogue to ease the situation.

▶ **PRACTICE 4**

Hilary: 'Jane, I feel very awkward about this but I haven't been clear in the past and we've got into a routine of travelling back together on Thursdays, which isn't always convenient to be honest.'

Jane: 'So what are you saying?'

Hilary: 'Well, would you mind if, in the future, we checked at the beginning of the class to see what our plans are?'

Jane: 'I don't see why not.'

Hilary: 'I'd really appreciate it if we could do that. I don't want to leave you in the lurch but sometimes I need to make other plans.'

Jane: 'You don't have to keep giving me a lift, you know. If it's easier we can just stop.'

Hilary: 'No, I'd be really happy to still give you a lift sometimes, honestly, but I'd like us to take it one evening at a time. Is that OK?'

Jane: 'That's fine. Thanks for ringing. See you Thursday then.'

Hilary: 'Look, Jane, before you go, I'd like to apologise, you know, for not saying anything earlier. It must be a bit of a surprise.'

Jane: 'Well, yes, it is actually. I'd assumed since you didn't say anything, that it was OK. I feel a bit awkward now, to be honest.'

Hilary: 'I would, too, in your position. Anyway, I can only say again that I'm sorry for not being clear. It really is not your fault at all. Thanks for being so understanding.'

Jane: 'That's OK.'

Hilary: 'I'll see you next week then. Bye.'

Jane: 'Bye.'

This is enough: to enquire as to the person's emotional response and to listen to their answer. You don't have to achieve a compulsory 'happy ending': all you can do is learn that dishonesty in relationships always causes suffering in the end.

When everyone depends on you

When you keep saying 'yes', other people come to rely on you. They depend on you, assuming you'll continue to behave in the way you always have done. They, of course, aren't to know that you aren't happy about this because you appear to be willing and amenable: you go along without complaint and get the tasks done. How could anyone guess that there is a whole knotted tangle of frustration inside which generates an internal conflict because you genuinely don't want to let people down, but also you realise that you have to set limits somewhere?

Nina and Terry

Nina is a single mother and likes to leave work on time to be back for her children. She is PA to Terry, who runs his own photographic agency. She enjoys her work but is frustrated with Terry's habit of leaving time-consuming tasks to the end of the day. He hands them to Nina, with a cheerful apology, and Nina rushes things through, putting herself through an awful lot of tension before she rushes home late.

The difficulty has several components: she is anxious about appearing inadequate to the task because she likes the work and doesn't want to lose her job. Terry is always so affable and is a nice boss so she finds it hard to let him down. However, she is also feeling anxious about her neighbour who takes in the children before she gets back: the woman is doing her a favour and is fine but Nina senses her annoyance from her when she has to phone and rearrange pickup time for an hour later.

Nina is certainly not unusual in trying to do the impossible. But the strain is beginning to tell on her health. She is getting bad headaches, not sleeping too well and getting snappy with the children. This is the effect not only of the physical tension of trying to cope with conflicting demands, but also the internal accumulation of unexpressed anger and desperation.

So how can she begin to set limits?

Her three answers are:

- Terry gives me work at the last minute

- I feel trapped

- I'd like him to organise his work more effectively

She has to confront an entrenched pattern in Terry's behaviour as well as her own inability to say no at the time when he hands her the work. This requires a two-pronged approach.

Taking responsibility for her own pattern of response means saying no more effectively. However, in the circumstances, Nina's anxiety at the moment of each request is overwhelming her.

The first part of this approach, then, is to set time aside to have a conversation with Terry, away from the actual moment he brings in the work to her.

Interestingly, even this first step can help or hinder the entire dialogue that follows.

Nina (putting her head round Terry's door): 'Oh, Terry. Have you got a minute? I need to talk to you about something.'

If Terry says he has got a minute, then Nina will start off rushed, unprepared and, most important, Terry won't have any idea that this 'minute' is actually very important to her.

Asking for enough time is part of taking ourselves seriously. Often when we're anxious, even when we need 30 minutes or an hour, we often ask only for 'a couple of minutes', which undermines the process from the very beginning.

Here Nina needs more than a minute: probably ten minutes would be the minimum to discuss this particular issue.

Consider the difference in this next dialogue:

Setting the scene: Nina goes into Terry's office and stands in front of him. He looks up at her.

Nina: 'Terry, there's something I'd like to discuss with you. It'll take 10–15 minutes. When would suit you?'

Terry: 'What's it about?'

Nina: 'I'd really rather wait to talk about it until we both have the time. When could we meet?'

Terry: 'Today?'

Nina: 'Yes, can we do it before 4 o'clock.'

Terry looks at his diary: '3.30 OK?'

Nina: 'Fine. I'll see you then.' (Exits.)

This illustrates a different approach but one that signals the importance of this conversation, somehow setting it *apart* from the other 95 per cent of their interaction. Why bother? Because to Nina it *is* important and the repercussions will be equally important for Terry as well.

Now comes the next part of dealing with Nina's problem.

Setting the scene: It's 3.30 and Nina enters Terry's office. She sits down.

> *Nina: 'Thanks for seeing me, Terry. This isn't easy for me, in fact, I'm quite anxious about bringing this up but I want to talk to you about the way you bring in work for me at the last minute.'*

> Terry smiles with recognition: 'I know. I never seem to get organised properly. It's all too hectic here.'

> *Nina: 'I know it is. And I don't want to let you down, which is what makes it really difficult for me to say no when you ask me to do stuff late. I'd really like us to come to some arrangement, say, that you give me whatever needs doing that day by 2 or 3 p.m. at the latest. You know I'm meant to leave here at 4.'*

> Terry: 'Well, you know me. I'll try but' (Shrugs his shoulders) 'it may just be impossible.'

Leaving it like this has given Nina an opportunity to air her problem but it has left her still dependent on Terry's ability to change. When he next gives her work at 3.45, Nina is unlikely to find it any easier to set clear limits. Often our own anxiety and fear of overstepping the mark make us hesitate to do so. It is one thing to ask Terry to change his behaviour, but to engage in more equal negotiation, she can set her own limits much more clearly. This is a vital aspect of personal power, even within a perpendicular system. Here's Practice 2:

▶ PRACTICE 2

Nina: 'Thanks for agreeing to see me, Terry. I'm anxious about bringing this up but it's important for me to find a solution. I've got a bit of a conflict of loyalties. You have a tendency to give me stuff to do just as I'm about to go home at 4 p.m. I find it hard to refuse you because I don't want to let you down but then I'm left caught between wanting to do my job properly and getting back for my family.'

Terry: 'So what are you suggesting?'

Nina: 'What I'd like, in future, is for you to get anything that needs doing the same day to me by 2 or 3 at the latest. If you can't do that, I'm going to have to say no to you. I don't know how you'd feel about that?'

Terry (a bit surprised): 'I hadn't realised that it was that difficult for you.' (He sighs) 'You know what it's like here.'

Nina: 'I know we're busy, which is why I'm telling you this in advance so that we can make some kind of contingency plan. Maybe we can ask Janice to help out or something. It's just that I need to leave on time.'

Terry (thoughtful): 'Well, I know I'm not the most organised person ... '

Nina: 'It would really help me if you could manage a 3 o'clock deadline. But if you can't, then can we ask Janice to help? Would you be happy with that?'

Terry: 'Yes, we'll see how it goes.'

Nina (getting up from the chair): 'Thanks for seeing me, Terry. I hope we can work it out.' (Exits.)

That's how Nina gets to a position of negotiation. Her heart may be pounding, her hands sweating, she may feel wrecked... but she got there. The gremlins will be having a field day warning her of all sorts of dire consequences for her boldness, but the likelihood is that this approach will pay dividends. Even when dealing with someone who has more status or authority, i.e. is above you on the ladder, you often have far more room to manoeuvre than you believe.

Chapter Twelve

Handling authority at work

There are two prevalent approaches to handling legitimate (hierarchical) power within any organisational structure: wielding it as a weapon or dropping it like a hot brick. Very few men or women appear to be able to balance their authority over others with a willingness also to negotiate with them. Some individuals hold back from wielding power over others, because they don't want to oppress them. However, it's easy to lose sight of the fact that we also oppress others when we neglect to set adequate boundaries for those for whom we are responsible, such as when we avoid taking responsibility or lack the courage to shelve our need to be liked when we have an unpleasant duty to perform. Dodging issues and fudging boundaries are just as much abuses of legitimate power as blatant exploitation: neither acknowledges the intrinsic equality of the person on the lower rung of the ladder. This is why it is crucial to handle our authority clearly.

Ben and the team

Ben is a director in a large bank. Three members of his department have been working for 18 months on a specific community project. They've put in a huge amount of work, planning and developing a special unit. Suddenly he has been told that the project has been axed: the powers that be have ordained that funds are no longer available.

It is his task to tell the team and he is dreading it because the unofficial head of the team, the prime mover, so to speak, is Wendy, a woman he doesn't much like. He finds her abrasive and difficult.

This is a classic opportunity to apply the hit and run approach described earlier in the situation between Hilary and Jane. He could send the news by e-mail and then be 'unavailable'. Or he could 'leak' the news so that they find out indirectly and then still make himself unavailable for comment.

It takes courage to be direct, but this is the only way to approach this kind of situation if we want to avoid oppression. One of the most common ways we oppress others – friends, children, clients, customers – is not simply by being authoritative or exercising legitimate power. It is what happens next that is crucial: whether or not we allow the other person to express their feelings *in response to our actions*. In our efforts to avoid and hide from having to deal with someone's legitimate hurt or anger, we deprive others of this right. This is one of the most common and 'normalised' examples of oppression that occurs in relationships where one person has power over the other.

So Ben decides to do the brave thing and sets up a meeting with the team in his office.

Setting the scene: The three women, Wendy, Mary and Trish arrive and sit down.

> Ben: 'Well ... thank you all for coming. I'm afraid I have some bad news, some very bad news actually.' (He feels the gaze of all three women upon him. He takes a breath.) 'I'm afraid the funding has been withdrawn from the project.'

> (In chorus): 'What??!!'

> Ben (his anxiety mounting): 'Yes. I heard yesterday and I was shocked. I'm sure you all are as well.'

> Wendy: 'I don't believe this. Why?'

> Ben: 'I don't know the details ...'

> Wendy: 'You mean you're not saying ...'

> Ben: 'No. I don't yet know the full story. I only know of this decision. I'm really sorry.'

> Wendy: 'Sorry? For heaven's sake, that really isn't good enough. Do you know how much work we've all put into this?' (The other two women nod in agreement.) 'I can't believe I'm hearing this,' she says turning to her team members. Suddenly she turns to Ben: 'Is this anything to do with you?'

> Ben (feeling irritated now): 'It's no good blaming me! My hands are tied. I've tried to be reasonable and I'm doing my best to be sympathetic but I think it's time to end this meeting.' (Stands up and makes a gesture towards the door with his arm.) 'Time to leave, ladies.'

They get up and go out. Wendy turns round at the door: 'You haven't heard the last of this, you know.'

Difficult Conversations

Ben sits down, fervently wishing he'd taken the easy way out. However, all Ben needs to do to improve his handling of this issue is to acknowledge the women's response. We easily feel threatened by the intensity of someone else's feelings and rush sometimes too quickly to put the lid on it all, to sweep it away before it gets 'out of control'. It's important for Ben to see that these women's feelings in this context are not merely an inconvenience that he doesn't want to deal with. They are real, understandable and they need *genuine* acknowledgement. Here's Practice 2:

▶ **PRACTICE 2**

Ben: 'Thank you all for coming.' (Takes a deep breath.) 'There's no way I can make this easy for any of us. This is very difficult but it's my task to give you some very, very bad news. The board have informed me that they have axed the project.'

(In chorus): 'What??!!'

Ben nods: 'I know. It is a huge shock. I was shocked just hearing the news and you're the ones who've been working on the whole thing so I can only imagine what you feel.'

Wendy: 'Why? I don't understand *why*.'

Ben shrugs: 'I don't know the reasons myself right now apart from a change of priority of funding.'

Wendy: 'Do you know how hard we've been working? It's all very well for you to sit there but we're the ones who've been slogging ourselves ...' (The others nod in agreement)

Ben: 'I am aware of that.'

Wendy looks at him suspiciously: 'Is it anything to do with you?'

Ben: 'No, it isn't.' (He looks directly at Wendy.) 'Look, I know you want someone to blame and shout at. I'd be the same in your position. It may make you feel better to have a go at me but unfortunately it won't alter the decision. It wasn't my decision.'

Mary: 'I just can't believe it.' (shaking her head in bewilderment).

Trish: 'I know ... I can't either.'

Wendy: 'Are you saying there's nothing we can do or you can do about this?'

Ben: 'Not at this moment.'

(Definitely time to close now.)

Ben: 'Look, it is a shock and I think it's best if we end this meeting here. I'll see if I can find out any more details and, if there is any chance of anything being changed, I'll let you know straightaway.'

He stands up: 'I really am very sorry to have to deliver such dreadful news to you all.' (The women gather their things and move towards the door.) 'I'll get back to you, I promise, when I find out more.'

We are never guaranteed happy endings, but Ben has handled this without being oppressive. He hasn't ducked his responsibility because of a fear of being disliked. He has been clear and direct and 'human'. This is an illustration of balancing both kinds of power, which is the challenge in the next scenario as well.

Alison and Mike

Alison is head of personnel working for local government. One of the training managers, Mike, never gets his monthly budget figures to her. Clearly she has the official authority to do this as part of her job but her personal power is affected by her response to this particular man. There is a definite spark between the two of them and she quite fancies him.

She has already been through the official process of explaining fully to him the need for a monthly return and that this is expected as part of his contract but nothing has changed. It is now at the stage where she is obliged to give him a verbal warning.

On the face of it, Alison's three answers are clear cut:

- Mike doesn't get his figures in

- I am frustrated

- I need to give him a verbal warning

Setting the scene: Alison calls Mike and sets up a meeting in her office.

Alison: 'Hi, Mike. Thanks for coming. Take a seat.'

Mike sits down: 'This is all rather formal isn't it?'

Alison: 'I have to talk to you about your refusal to get your budget figures in each month.'

Mike: 'Have I been a bad boy again?'

Alison: 'Look, Mike ... this is serious.'

Mike smiles at her in such a way that she can feel herself going weak at the knees.

Alison (struggling): 'Mike, I have to give you a verbal warning.'

Mike: 'My God, has it come to that already?'

Alison: 'I'm afraid so.'

Mike: 'Can't you give me another chance? I am trying you know. You got them in May, didn't you?'

Alison (smiling in spite of herself): 'Yes, they did come in May but not since.'

Mike: 'Look, I know you're just doing your job and I really admire you for that but can't you just this once let it go. I promise you I'll make every effort ... you'll see.'

Alison (succumbing to his charm): 'I don't know, Mike. I have to do my job, you know.'

Mike: 'You are doing your job, very well. All I'm saying is that I am taking on board what you're saying and I will improve. Trust me.' (Looks deep into her eyes.)

Alison doesn't know what to say. She hesitates.

Mike: 'Look, wait until the end of this month and you'll see, I'll get them in on time. OK?'

Alison gives in.

When he's gone, she is left feeling very uncomfortable. She knows she should have been firmer but perhaps he may improve. Surely she should give him this last chance?

The issue here is one of boundaries. Most of us need to be liked but this need can get in the way of keeping clear boundaries, which are necessary both to maintain personal power and also to exercise legitimate power. Alison is going to have to choose a priority: her work or her personal need to be considered 'attractive' to someone she rather fancies. It is very hard because we're all susceptible. But if she goes with her need to please Mike, she'll not fulfil her responsibilities. If she makes her work the priority, and settling in this context for respect, she has a chance of coming across more authoritatively.

▶ **PRACTICE 2**

Alison: 'Hi, Mike. Do take a seat.'

Mike: 'What have I done this time?'

Alison: 'This is difficult for me, Mike, but this meeting is to give you a verbal warning. I'm extremely frustrated about this because you are a very able trainer but you know that supplying the budget figures are part of your contract here.'

Mike: 'It can't have to come to that already.'

Alison: 'I'm afraid it has and this is why I have to give you a verbal warning.'

Mike: 'You got them in May. Come on, why don't you just give me until the end of this month. I promise you I'll improve.' (Looks into her eyes.)

Alison looks back at Mike very directly: 'Mike, as I've said, this isn't an easy task. I'm genuinely sorry but it's my job to do this because you've ignored all my other requests and the procedure is clearly set down. You know that.'

Mike (in a somewhat seductive tone): 'You're being very firm with me, aren't you?'

(Time to close.)

Alison (keeping it very formal): 'We need to end it there, Mike. I hope you can use this warning to improve. We'd be sad to lose you. You're an excellent trainer.' (Stands up and goes to the door to open it for Mike.)

Alison's professional boundary is a helpful reminder to her. Keeping the interaction formal gives her a chance to put her attraction aside and retain a measure of independence. This is another aspect of personal power: being willing, at times, to put aside our need to be liked and to settle for knowing we are doing our work with integrity.

Chapter Thirteen

Enemy or equal?

As we become more familiar with and more established within our own personal power, the ability to balance it with perpendicular power becomes easier. As this happens, we see more clearly how it profoundly affects our attitude to others. It affects especially the way in which we normally jump to the conclusion that any kind of conflict means the other person is automatically the *enemy*.

The anticipation of aggression leads us to see the other person as the opposition, as a competitor or rival for the position of winner. This is a hard habit to break. Even if we're convinced of the importance of personal power and equality in theory, the moment we encounter an offensive colleague or a totally unhelpful shop assistant in reality, we immediately find ourselves convinced that the offence is deliberate. This 'conviction' instantly fuels the counter-response of blame.

If and when you decide that you're going to shelve aggression, you have to re-image the other person. You literally have to make the effort to see the other person differently. On top of the image of the annoying neighbour, the loathsome boss, the

... the shop assistant is not your enemy

bullying colleague, you have to see an image of a human being. If you can do this, you will certainly be going against the 'norm' but what happens, intriguingly, is that you'll often find that once you stop *seeing* someone as an enemy, they stop behaving like one.

Kate and her neighbour

Kate is a masseuse and is working with clients on a sunny Saturday afternoon when some neighbours start playing very loud music. Her first response is irritation: how inconsiderate people are/it's so selfish/how can she possibly be expected to provide a calm environment for her clients with that racket outside?

Her anger is understandable because anger is a healthy emotional response to the invasion of our boundaries. Noise, like other forms of pollution, is increasingly invasive. Noise is fine when you're in the middle of it but not when you're on the outside. When noise intrudes, an invisible barrier is broken: your own private space is invaded.

Kate's first impulse is to yell down at the perpetrators in the basement flat next door from her fifth floor roof terrace. This would allow her to express some fury at a safe distance from retaliation: she's already into battle mode. Then she realises that from this distance, her yells (from a height) are likely to be provocative and probably they won't take any notice anyway.

This kind of scenario presents us always with a choice. Does it matter? Can I live with it or would I really like to do something about it? If we decide to do something about it, then it follows that if we're going to go to all that bother, we'd like a good result. Either we go for strong-arm tactics to guarantee victory or we try a strategy that will give us the best chance of communicating our request and having it heard.

None of us listens when threatened, attacked, patronised or made to feel inferior. Our eyes and ears close down as we go into survival mode. It follows therefore that if we want to communicate something important to someone else and we would like to be heard and acknowledged, we should slip out of our battle gear and leave it behind.

Adopting this approach means you'll often discover that, contrary to your assumption, the other person doesn't know how their behaviour is affecting you. This dialogue then becomes a process of informing them of its effect on you and asking for a change or compromise. The majority of people will respond co-operatively.

Of course, a minority will not. Then, depending on the circumstances, you can resort to more official strategies. But it is worth trying this approach first ... just to see. It doesn't always mean you'll get what you want, but you'll multiply your chances a thousandfold by giving the other person a chance instead of assuming their 'guilt' before you start.

Kate considers going to visit her neighbours. She is nervous because she doesn't know them but she steels herself and goes downstairs to the next door house.

Her three answers are:

- I am disturbed by the noise and trying to work
- I'm frustrated
- I would like them to turn the music down, preferably off

Kate rings what appears to be the basement bell. No response. The music's too loud she tells herself. She bangs on the door. She considers giving up and going back. She only has half an hour before her next client. She gives one more loud bang on the door and hears footsteps approaching. It opens and a young man stares at her, a little the worse for wear.

Kate: 'I'd like to speak to someone about the music.'

He goes off without a word. The door stays open.

Kate waits a couple of minutes. She then shouts 'Hello' quite loudly.

A girl appears. She says crossly: 'Yes?'

Kate: 'Hi. I feel awkward asking you this but I live next door and have to work all this afternoon. At the moment your music is really doing my head in and I'd appreciate it if you could turn the volume down.'

Neighbour (with pained expression): 'It's too hot to have the windows closed. It's the weekend ... it's not my fault if you're working.'

> *Kate: 'It is hot. Look, I know it's not your fault and I don't want to spoil your fun but I have to work on Saturdays. All I'm asking is that we compromise a little, please.'*

> Neighbour sighs: 'I'll see what I can do.' (Goes in and shuts the door.)

Kate shrugs her shoulders and goes back inside. Ten minutes later, the music goes down a little. She would have liked it off altogether but realises she can only achieve so much in this particular situation. What she has proved to herself, though, is that the myth that everyone is your natural enemy is not true.

It becomes impossible to move in any interaction as long as we insist on seeing the other as enemy. This is the whole point of this model of communication. We can be aggressive and vengeful and patronising, get a real buzz from competition and aggression and a great high from actual conquest. But in terms of reciprocal communication, not a command from on high, we have to make a major mental shift and imagine a human being alongside the 'monster', the 'completely selfish bastard' or the 'fundamentally nasty piece of work'.

Clare and Dave

Clare is head of human resources and has received complaints of substandard behaviour regarding one of the directors, Tim. She has passed them on to Dave, the CEO, but he hasn't done anything because Tim's a buddy of his and so nothing has gone any further. She's aware that Dave is stalling but almost can't be bothered to say anything to him. She finds him incompetent, arrogant, she doesn't trust him, she hates the croneyism, he's sexist, he's everything . . . in short she despises him.

She would like to say something but without causing a fight. She has therefore to stop seeing him as the enemy; otherwise this process is a non-starter.

Clare prearranges a meeting. Her three answers are:

- Dave isn't dealing with the complaints
- I feel furious and helpless
- I'd like him to deal with it

Clare enters Dave's office.

> Clare: *'Dave, this is not an easy situation for me.'*

Dave looks and waits.

> Clare: *'I want to keep this short and to the point. I've had complaints about Tim's behaviour, as you know, and it appears that you haven't passed them on. I'd like to know why.'*

Dave (bristling): 'I don't know what you're talking about. I did my own investigation and, as far as I could find, the complaints were unfounded. I suggest you look elsewhere before you start accusing me of something you might regret.' (He gives her a long, threatening look.)

The daggers are now drawn between them. Clare is aware of both her nervousness and her loathing for the man in front of her. Clare will have to fight or back off . . . or she can disarm.

She decides to leave the battle and moves into a base of personal power.

> Clare (takes a deep breath): *'Dave. I don't want to have a fight with you. You're my boss so there wouldn't be much point.*

> *All I want to say is that three members of staff have com-plained separately about Tim. I pass the complaints on to you but nothing happens. What I would like is for you to deal with those complaints appropriately. It is nothing to do with me personally. I am asking only for the sake of the whole depart-ment. That's what is important to me, and that alone. Until you do something, we are going to continue to have prob-lems that are doing us a lot of harm.' (She stands up.) 'I'd like you to think about it, Dave. I won't take up any more of your time.'*

> *She faces him: 'Thank you for seeing me.' (Exits).*

Clare will never like her boss but she's been able to state what she wanted and then to make a clean and unencumbered get-away. That was a truly empowering move for her. Dave may not change but Clare can live with her own integrity intact.

When we're stuck rigidly with the image of an enemy who has more (perpendicular) power than ourselves, we're also stuck on the 'lower' rung, seeing ourselves as helpless to do anything about what is happening to us. Ridding ourselves of the perception of the enemy means the possibility of one small step towards change.

Scott and his colleagues

Scott is desperately wishing he were much taller and that he possessed the physique and powers of Superman, so that he could wreak horrible but just revenge on his tormentors at work.

He is in his twenties and a qualified chef in a busy hotel kitchen. It's already his third job because he hates the hassle: he isn't high up the rungs of the ladder but he isn't at the bottom either and yet he finds it impossible to deal with his fellow chefs. He starts on one job and is then told to do another and everyone seems to enjoy bullying him. It makes him utterly miserable.

Scott can keep wishing he were a different sort of person, with a different sort of temperament, but in truth, he's shy and reserved and not naturally extrovert. He cannot change who he is but he can choose to start setting limits once he sorts out what is happening.

Setting the scene: Scott is chopping parsley when Michel comes up and dumps a sack of potatoes by his side.

Michel: 'Get on with these. I need them immediately.'

Scott: 'But, I've got this to finish ... '

Michel (glowers): 'You do as I say. Right?' (Goes off.)

Five minutes later, Gary comes up with another bunch of herbs and slaps them on the counter: 'We need those in the next five minutes ... ' and so it goes on.

From the bullied position, Scott cannot move. He can resent and detest but he cannot move. His fantasies take him into the upper position, with himself as the bully, reversing the positions. But he has to get off the ladder completely if he is to alter his situation. He has to consider himself as an equal, regardless of how others are treating him.

- What are the others doing? Not letting him finish one job before he has to start another

- How does he feel currently? Frustrated and furious

- What does he want? To set limits

▶ **PRACTICE 2**

Scott is once again chopping parsley. Michel comes up with a load of potatoes.

Michel: 'Get on with these. I need them now.' (Starts to walk away.)

Scott: 'Michel. I need to finish this job first for Jake. I can't start on the potatoes for another ten minutes. Is that OK?

Michel: 'What the fuck are you on about? I said right now.'

Scott (maintaining direct eye contact): 'I'm sorry, Michel. I can't do them now. I have to finish the parsley. If you can wait five minutes, I'll be glad to do them.'

Michel looks extremely put out but goes away.

Scott continues to chop. He's incredibly nervous and relieved that nobody can see how much he's sweating. One encounter like this is often a watershed in the life of someone who's been frequently bullied. Now he knows he can do it again.

Gary approaches with several lettuces: 'I need these washed pronto.'

Scott: 'Sure, Gary. I will do them as soon as I've finished this and the potatoes' (indicating the sack) 'for Michel. Probably 20 minutes? Can you wait or do you want to find someone else?'

Gary looks totally incredulously at Scott but as there is no aggression at all coming *from* Scott to latch on to, he can only feel disgruntled and flounces off with a prima donna toss of his head.

With one encounter at a time Scott can challenge the peremptory orders of the others, proving he doesn't have to be pushed around. This is what personal power is all about: get rid of the enemy in your sights and instead of getting stuck in the 'under' position because you have no hope of being 'over', get off the ladder. Visualise yourself and the other as *equal*. Then you can make some clear moves towards improving the reality of your situation.

Chapter Fourteen

Equality in relationship

Probably the easiest relationship in which to maintain a sense of equality is friendship: the dynamics of friendship at any age are naturally based in equality. Negotiating equality in any relationship where there is a predisposed hierarchy of age, position, status and so on makes it more difficult. We are greatly affected by the social ladders that surround us even when they're invisible. Sometimes this is no more than a desire to be courteous and polite. Sometimes it's a genuine choice to put someone else's needs first. But at other times, it becomes such an automatic response that even when equality is possible, we don't take the opportunity to claim it.

In intimate relationships, the power over/power under dynamic is still often the one that dominates. Even within the apparent equality of modern relationships, many women in heterosexual relationships still have a tendency to behave in ways that suggest they feel in some way *un*equal when it comes to dealing with conflicting needs.

Personal power is something we can hold on to or give away. In intimate relationships, many women of all ages find themselves trapped in a situation that they have helped to maintain by failing to assert their own equality. Women often hesitate to disagree openly and instead, keep quiet, going along with things instead of speaking out. When push comes to shove, fear of conflict creates such dread that many lack the courage and resources to stand firm and stay clear.

How do you claim your own personal power in a relationship? You have to make a decisive choice to give up the winner/loser system of conflict. You have to open your eyes to the possibility that conflict doesn't have to lead to a fight but an exploration of the differences between you and your partner. Conflict doesn't have to represent a major rift: sometimes it arises when we are faced with a difference of opinion or desire. Achieving a point of negotiation means being clear about the answers to all three questions.

One of the most frequent complaints women make about men is that they don't want to talk about feelings. Certainly, for reasons of their own conditioning, many men are less comfortable with expressing their feelings but what gets lost from view is the large part that women play in being very unclear about their own feelings in the first place. Women pride themselves on being more emotionally attuned but this rarely entails clarity. A woman often gets herself into an emotional stew so that a simple request becomes bogged down in a whole lot of other feelings because of a backlog of other things that haven't been addressed. On the receiving end, a man who is perhaps uneasy, then starts trying to understand an apparently simple issue only to find himself embroiled in much deeper emotional territory and having to dodge barbs and attacks that seem to come out of nowhere!

Instead of complaining about men's emotional inarticulacy, women also have the option of learning to specify exactly what they actually want and to be a lot clearer about their own emotional tangle. Specifically, this entails the possibility of risking open, clear statements instead of trying to control the outcome of the conversation by manipulation. When women depend too much on trying to keep the peace, it becomes hard to maintain emotional independence: this leads to all sorts of problems in relationships.*

Chrissie and Jed

Chrissie and Jed live together and Jed has announced that his best friend from university days, Mike, who moved to Australia, wants to come and stay for three months while he does a project in the UK. Jed has e-mailed back that it's fine, presuming that Chrissie wouldn't object. After all it's only for three, at the most, four months.

Chrissie isn't happy but is not sure why. She's tried to explain this to Jed but he's not taken her seriously: he thinks she's miffed that he didn't ask her first, for which he has already apologised.

After a lot of thought, Chrissie is clear about her three answers:

● Jed wants Mike to come and stay

● I feel unhappy

● I would like him to make other arrangements

Going through this process, she has realised why she doesn't want Mike there. She's met him only once and she doesn't really like him. She certainly doesn't want him staying for so long.

---

* If you are interested in following up on these issues of women and relationship you can read more in my book, *A Voice for Now*.

On top of everything else, their flat is small and Mike would have to take the one spare room that she likes to use. It gives her a bit of space away from everything at the end of a busy day.

Once she's realised *why*, she feels convinced that she should tell Jed. She's aware that this could be labelled selfish but she doesn't want to have months of feeling cramped.

Setting the scene: She arranges to talk to Jed early evening.

> *Chrissie: 'Jed, can I talk to you about something?'*

> Jed: 'What?'

> *Chrissie: 'I've been thinking about Mike coming and I still don't feel happy about it.'*

> Jed: 'Oh come on, Chrissie, I thought we'd been through all that once.'

> *Chrissie: 'But I didn't explain it was because I don't want to feel so cramped. He'd have to have the spare room and I use that. And I don't really like him that much.'*

> Jed: 'Don't you think you're being a bit selfish about this? I mean, it's only for a few months. It's not for ever. He's my best mate and he's done me a lot of favours. There's no reason why he can't come here. That's the end of it. End of story. I'm going out.' (Gets up and leaves.)

Chrissie is furious and tearful. She feels completely ignored. Chrissie realises that she's angry because Jed's steamrollering over her.

What's going on for Jed? He's probably not aware that he's bullying her: he's worried about how it would look if he has to tell Mike he can't stay and the effect on their friendship so his attitude is likely to stem from wanting to avoid any hassle for himself. His friendship with Mike is important to him but has Chrissie expressed how important her own needs are?

Chrissie reflects on how important this is to her. Is she prepared to go along with what Jed wants or not? She concludes that because it matters a great deal to her, if all else fails, she'll find somewhere else to stay.

▶ **PRACTICE 2**

Chrissie: 'Jed, I want to talk about our disagreement about Mike coming.'

Jed: 'I told you that was the end of the story.'

Chrissie (in a strong voice): 'No, Jed, don't shut me up like that. I wasn't clear before and it's not the end of the story. Our relationship means everything to me but it has to be on an equal footing. You can't simply ignore my needs by pretending they don't exist. I know it's important for you to have Mike to stay. It's also important for me to have some space. There are two of us living here and I'd like you to see both our views as equal. Then we can look at how we reach some kind of compromise.'

Jed (struck by her forcefulness, but not defensive): 'How do you mean?'

Chrissie: 'I don't know how to resolve it. I'd like us to find a solution together instead of you not listening to me.'

Jed: 'You are being totally unreasonable.'

Chrissie: 'Jed! Stop telling me I'm wrong because I disagree with you.'

There's a silence.

Chrissie: 'Oh, Jed. I promise you I'm not just being petty and unreasonable. That room is really important to me – it's like a little haven. I don't want to live in a cramped space with someone I don't feel that comfortable with. I know you don't want to let Mike down so I'm even prepared to move out myself.'

Jed (taken aback): 'Don't be so ridiculous.'

Chrissie smiles: 'I mean it!'

Jed relaxes a little and shakes his head: 'So what are we going to do then?'

They've reached a point where they can negotiate because both are fully aware of each other's conflicting needs. They can now focus their energy on finding a solution *together*.

Katrina and Neil

Handling conflicting needs in close relationships always requires you to be clear about what you want. Katrina and Neil are getting married in six months' time and they both want a fairly conventional wedding. A conflict has already arisen between Katrina and her father. Her mother died several years ago and her father has remarried Sheila, who has two daughters from a previous marriage. Sheila is very keen to have these two girls, aged 14 and 16, as bridesmaids at the coming wedding. Katrina is ambivalent but Neil is adamant that he doesn't want all that fuss.

So poor Katrina is caught in the middle. She is trying unsuccessfully to persuade Neil to incorporate two bridesmaids into the scheme of things; trying to avoid Sheila's phone calls; trying to think of a way to be tactful in the face of her father's quiet pressure to accommodate Sheila and the girls.

This is precisely the kind of muddle we get ourselves into when trying to balance everyone's needs and keep them happy. What disappears from view is the answer to that third question: What do *I* want?

Katrina must ask herself this first if she is to find a way through. After some thought, she realises that what is most important to her isn't just a questions of bridesmaids or no bridesmaids. What she wants more than anything is for Neil and herself to be in full agreement. She doesn't want to start off their whole marriage on the wrong foot.

Her first move is to sit down with Neil and discuss it over coffee.

Katrina: 'Neil, there's something I want to talk to you about. It's about the bridesmaid question.'

Neil groans.

Katrina: 'I need you to listen to me! At the moment, I feel caught up between everyone else and I'm feeling desperate. So I want to know how dead set against bridesmaids you are. I mean, would you consider them at all?'

Neil: 'I've said before and I'll say it again that I don't want a traditional wedding with all the trimmings. Just sort it out with your family.'

Katrina: 'So you're absolutely against the idea, then.'

Neil: 'Katrina!'

Katrina: 'All right, I just wanted to be sure. You see, I don't actually mind to be honest.'

Neil looks at her, open-mouthed.

Neil's belligerence is a typical response to the kind of hedging and indirectness of Katrina's approach. She now wonders where to go from here. What does she feel? She feels very alone with it all. Realising this, she then sees what it is she wants.

She looks at Neil: 'I'm in the middle of this, because it's my family. But I'd like your help. If you and I agree that we are saying no to the girls, then I want both of us to go there and say so. I don't mind speaking but I want you there too. I don't think it's fair that I should have to do this on my own.'

Neil: 'It is your family. I don't have any part of it.'

Katrina: 'Neil, if we're getting married, you will be part of it. And I'd like to start by you and I seeing this as a shared problem, not just mine.'

Neil: 'In what way?'

Katrina: 'Well, even if they're not bridesmaids, can we make it a special occasion for the girls too, you know, give them some part to play? I'd really like us to find a compromise.'

It takes a lot of courage to speak up. You have to find a measure of emotional independence to balance your own needs with those of someone you love. This is how personal power can help you in times of fear and confusion. Consistently focusing on a way through, which your three answers will give you, helps you to get beyond the anxiety of conflict. Without it, you'll easily fall prey to inertia and prevarication, and then risk getting stuck in feeling powerless.

Maeve and George

Maeve and George have been married over 40 years. As September approaches, Maeve is wondering how to get out of the annual trip to the international military brass band festival. She loves George but secretly hates brass band music. Because she's been doing something she doesn't enjoy for so long, she now hates the whole trip. The journey, the hotel, dinner in the evening, everything is soured.

Three weeks before, she complains of feeling a bit unwell. George is concerned for her and their forthcoming trip. What can she do? To speak up now will reveal more than she wants to reveal. And yet, she can feel everything in her body tensing in resistance.

Maeve's three answers are:

● George expects me to go to the festival

● I don't enjoy it

● I have to tell him I don't want to go

Setting the scene: She decides to take her courage in both hands after dinner.

Maeve: *'George, love, I want to say something.'*

George: 'Go on then.'

Maeve: *'I don't really want to go to the festival this year.'*

George (incredulous): 'Why not?'

Maeve: *'I don't feel like it this year.'*

George: 'What's different this year? We always have a good time.'

Maeve: *'I'd really rather not go.'*

George: 'We've got everything booked now.'

Maeve: *'Oh, dear!'*

She can't ignore the past. Maeve has to acknowledge her own inability to balance her own needs with George's and come clean. Here's Practice 2.

▶ **PRACTICE 2**

Maeve: *'George, love, I've got a bit of a confession to make.'*

George: 'My God, what is it?'

Maeve *(smiles seeing the shocked expression on his face): 'It's all right. Listen, I'm embarrassed saying this but it really is a confession. You know, all these years, we've gone to the brass band festival and do you know what, I really hate it.'*

George: 'You don't!'

Maeve: *'I do. I really don't like the music at all.'*

George: 'So why've you never said?'

Maeve: *'I couldn't. I didn't want to disappoint you. It's my own fault. I'm not blaming you at all. I just kept quiet but it's got to the stage now where I dread the thought of it.'*

George is shaking his head in disbelief. 'I can't believe you never said. You always seemed to be enjoying it. I don't understand.'

Maeve: 'I know, it must be a bit of a shock. I'm sorry just to drop it on you like this. I love being with you, just not the music.'

George: 'What are we going to do then?'

Maeve: 'I don't know. I'm happy if you want to go on your own ... or you could take someone else.'

George: 'Who?!'

Maeve: 'I don't know. Maybe, er ... Graham?'

George: 'Wouldn't be the same without you. Anyway, I've booked the hotel and everything.'

Maeve: 'For this year, yes. Well, this year I could come with you but do something else. I could do some sightseeing or shopping. I'd quite enjoy that and we could meet up in between. How would that be?'

George (disappointed and still digesting this revelation): 'I suppose so.'

(Time to close.)

Maeve: 'Come on, go and put the kettle on. Or should we go down to the club? We need a drink. I do anyway!'

Without blame and by asserting the equality of your needs, you stop handing over your personal power and then eventually resenting it. Equal negotiation takes committment but leaves no nasty little piles of resentment to fester.

Chapter Fifteen

Having the courage to speak up

When we wisely keep quiet at certain times, we retain our self-respect. When we keep quiet, though, through persistent fear, our personal power is diminished. Sometimes it is an aggressive response that we fear. This persuades us to turn a blind eye and a deaf ear to all sorts of behaviour that we don't feel comfortable with, even when we do need to confront it. Even in an extremely difficult situation like the one below, where there seems to be *no* right thing to say, there are still ways to set up a situation so the risks of it turning into an unpleasant altercation are minimised.

Jack and a difficult client

Jack and Simon are driving to what they know will be a difficult meeting. Simon is a senior social worker in child protection, Jack a recently qualified member of his team. They have been asked to make a visit to Susan, John and their family because there has been a request for financial assistance and for the family to be moved to larger accommodation.

The two men face a professional dilemma. Susan has three small children, all under nine, living with her and has recently started a relationship with John, who has a teenaged daughter by a previous relationship. This girl has reported to a different authority that she has been physically and sexually abused by her father. Obviously there is grave cause for concern but there hasn't been enough time to investigate or substantiate these allegations, which could prove to be unreliable. What aggravates the situation for these two men is that John is reputed to be highly confrontational and easily provoked to violence.

Theoretically, the social workers have power *over* the couple, but their position is undermined by the current lack of proof: they don't want to risk being sued for wrongful accusation. How can they broach the subject without falling foul of John's temper? They have to make this visit but their dilemma is whether to stick to the request for assistance or to confront the much more pressing subject of the allegation in view of there being three small children in the house.

At the meeting, fear wins and nothing is said. In the car travelling back to the office, Simon justified his failure to speak up by reasoning that there were no obvious signs of abuse and the children didn't seem unduly frightened of John so he decided to wait until the burden of proof was absolute. Jack is uncomfortable. He felt too junior to speak up at the time and deferred to Simon who had felt intimidated and consequently had pussyfooted around the whole issue.

Lack of confrontation doesn't only affect us as individuals: it can have serious ramifications throughout many people's lives. It happens in professional contexts because there is no training to give individuals the appropriate skills but, in this situation, it is also part of a much wider tendency to silence. If you consider the storm that arises when it finally emerges, for example, that children have been abused in an establishment over a period of years, we have only to remember that there are always other adults around who are not involved in the abuse but who suspect, are uneasy, uncomfortable about what they think is or may be happening, but fear keeps them locked into tacit denial and therefore collusion.

Each one of us has at some time witnessed abusive or questionable behaviour towards another person and kept quiet. We want to avoid trouble. Sometimes we are relieved that the aggression isn't directed towards ourselves; sometimes we don't think we'd be believed; we tell ourselves it's none of our business. Either way, fear is a powerful inhibitor and with our culture becoming increasingly litigious, there is even more 'reason' in professional contexts to keep quiet.

Jack decides he wants to have another go. He can't stop feeling regret about the meeting and is concerned for the children in the house. He checks with his supervisor who is dubious but agrees to Jack going back, as long as he is careful to follow the standard guidelines for the situation.

Jack's three answers are:

- There's been an allegation of sexual abuse

- I feel very concerned about the future of the children here

- If our investigation finds the allegation to be true, the children may well be taken into care

Setting the scene: Jack arranges another meeting. He takes a colleague, Steve, but intends to do the talking himself. He rings the bell. Susan opens the door.

Jack: 'Hello, Susan. How are you? This is my colleague, Steve. Is John around? I'd like to talk to you both together.'

139

The two men go into the lounge and wait for John to come downstairs. When he does, the four of them sit down.

Jack: 'I'm here this morning with something very difficult to say to you both.'

They look at him and wait.

Jack: 'We've had an allegation against you, John (looks at him) of abuse, physical and sexual abuse, and we are duty bound to look into it.'

John (instantly defensive): 'Who's made the allegation?'

Jack: 'I'm not at liberty to talk about that, John. I'm sure you must both be very shocked by this information but I can't discuss it with you until we know more about it.'

John (angrily): 'You can't just accuse me of something ... '

Jack: 'John, I realise this is a shock to you but it is my responsibility to inform you because, unfortunately, there will be implications for your children here, Susan.'

Susan: 'You'll take them away.'

Jack: 'Yes, Susan. If there is truth in this then we'll have to take them into care for their own safety. I'm sure you'd want that yourself.'

Susan: 'But you're not saying it's true yet.'

Jack: 'No, I'm telling you that we've had allegations that we have to pursue.'

(Time to close.)

Jack stands up and his colleague follows suit.

Jack's face is grave: 'I'm sorry it was my duty to bring you this news.'

John stands up too: 'You can't just make accusations and walk out of here!'

Jack: 'I can say nothing else right now, John, but I promise I'll phone you and arrange for a meeting in the office so that you can both come and find out what's happening. I'll ring you before the end of this week.'

Turns and goes towards the front door. He opens it and the two colleagues step into the road and walk towards the car.

On the way back to the office, Jack feels wiped out by it all. He laughs now as he shares with Steve how terrified he was but Steve assures him it didn't show. Jack has handled a tricky situation with tact and also managed to avoid provoking aggression. His promise to keep them posted and ring them is important because in showing a concern for them, he avoids the hit and run approach. These apparently small aspects of consideration in a difficult encounter make a huge difference; they reverberate in the same way as aggression reverberates, but, in this instance, they leave no trail of damage.

On a smaller scale, in less dramatic circumstances, we can all practise speaking out when we witness obvious unpleasantness happening to someone else. Obviously we have to be careful not to put ourselves at risk of physical harm but there are many instances where, if we're really honest, we're afraid of nothing worse than a bit of disapproval.

Alex, Sharon and Gary

Alex feels uncomfortable whenever she is out together with Sharon, her friend, and Sharon's boyfriend Gary. Gary has a habit of putting Sharon down in public, and Sharon seems to tolerate it with good humour, although Alex wonders how she really feels. She's asked Sharon about it but Sharon replied that it was 'just his way'. So Alex has said nothing but she hasn't stopped feeling uncomfortable. Her three answers are:

- Gary puts Sharon down

- I don't like it

- I'd like him to stop

They're out for a drink. Gary is once again teasing Sharon about being stupid. Alex finds herself alone with Gary while Sharon has gone to the loo so she decides to use the opportunity.

> Alex: *'Gary, I feel a bit awkward about saying this but why do you keep putting Sharon down? You keep making out she's thick or making her feel awful about putting on weight.'*
>
> Gary: *'It's a laugh, that's all.'*
>
> Alex: *'It's not funny though, is it, really?'*
>
> Gary (looks quite threateningly at her): *'I really don't think it's any of your business.'*
>
> They see Sharon coming back and stop talking.

Alex has found the courage to speak up but needs to be very clear about her bottom line. Your bottom line means: how far are you prepared to put up with a situation if nothing is going to change? Is Alex prepared to let it go? How much does it matter to her? She can't speak up on Sharon's behalf as Sharon is an adult and must find her own voice. So Alex is expressing a limit for herself but she's not the one in the relationship. But, as Alex thinks this through, she realises that if Gary takes no notice of what she says, then it *does* become her business ... as long as she stays around the two of them. Here's Practice 2.

▶ **PRACTICE 2**

Alex: 'Gary, look I feel awkward saying this but I feel really uncomfortable when you put Sharon down – you know about her being stupid or getting fat.'

Gary: 'She doesn't mind.'

Alex: 'I don't know if that's true but I don't like it. It sounds really unkind.'

Gary: 'Look. I think it's your problem, not Sharon's. It really is none of your business, you know.'

Sharon is making her way back and detects the silence.

Sharon: 'So, what are you two talking about?'

Gary: 'Nothing. Nothing at all.'

Alex: 'Sharon, that's actually not true. I told Gary that I didn't like the way he kept putting you down about your weight and stuff and he basically told me to mind my own business.'

Sharon: 'Oh dear, he doesn't mean anything ... '

Alex (realises her bottom line): 'Maybe it isn't my business, but I don't have to stay around and listen.'

Sharon: 'You're not going ... ?!'

Alex (looking directly at Sharon): 'Yes, I am going. I don't enjoy listening to you being slagged off, I really don't. I'll give you a ring in the next couple of days. Bye.'

Not an easy exit for her but Alex has set her limits and feels more comfortable than she would living with the uneasy compromise of tacit collusion. This is the kind of choice you sometimes have to deal with when you want to hold on to your own integrity.

The bottom line

Our bottom line presents us with a fundamental question: what happens if you describe the behaviour, express your feelings, state clearly what you'd like to be different, in other words, put yourself through this entire process and ... nothing changes. In other words, the individual will not alter their behaviour either because they can't or won't. This represents a very different scenario from one in which someone doesn't agree to change what they're doing simply because you haven't communicated your feelings clearly enough. This time, even with the insight into how their behaviour affects *you*, there is no wish or agreement to act otherwise.

This is when you need to think things through very carefully. How important is this problem? *Does it matter if nothing changes?* Can I live quite happily with the trail of dirty socks or constant insults? Deep down, do I privately go along with the situation as it is, even though I moan and complain about it? These are personal and individual questions that nobody can answer for anyone else. What are my real limits? Am I prepared to put up with my husband's behaviour and stay in this relationship? Do I stay in this job even though they refuse to pay me appropriately? Can I still be part of this friendship if I cannot trust her? Do I continue to support my daughter even if she refuses to take some responsibility for her life? Your bottom line tells you the limit of what you are prepared to tolerate in any given situation.

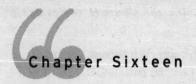

Chapter Sixteen

Love has its limits

It's important to remember that we always have a choice. In fact, we usually have a few different options available to us, even if we don't want to act on them. It comes down to deciding how important a particular issue is in your life. Does it matter? How much? You can ask yourself this each time. Sometimes it doesn't matter, sometimes it does. Sometimes you kid yourself it doesn't matter only to find that you're sitting on a pile of resentment, which clearly says otherwise.

Whether the issue is major or minor, you have a choice of response. The recognition of having reached a point beyond which you're not prepared to go – your personal bottom line – can be a painfully confronting experience. You then have to find the courage to face this reality and deal with the fact that you know you've had enough.

Will and Sandy

Will and Sandy, both in their thirties, have been together for seven years. Will has a problem with Sandy's drinking. Over the years, they've had rows then reconciliations, more rows and more reconciliations but nothing has changed. He has suggested she get help but after a few visits to a counsellor, Sandy declared she was not an alcoholic, merely a social drinker.

He loves her when she's sober. He cares for her very deeply but he can't (doesn't want to) take the strain any more. He wants to ask her one more time if she will get treatment because he is clear that he has arrived at his bottom line: unless she takes her alcoholism seriously, he wants to end the relationship.

Obviously it is easy for the bottom line to be seen as a threat (aggression), so it's important how we communicate in these circumstances. Will's three answers are:

- Sandy is drinking too much and won't accept she has a problem

- I feel frustrated and desperate

- I'd like her to commit herself for proper treatment for alcoholism

Setting the scene: It goes without saying that this conversation needs to take place when Sandy is completely sober. This applies to everyone who wants to use this process properly, even those who don't have a problem with alcohol. Starting off under the influence of any chemical substance will mean that you don't fully experience the anxiety that is quite natural and normal and what you communicate will be distorted as a consequence.

So Will decides to make the time to talk to Sandy while they are out walking one afternoon.

Will: 'Sandy, there's something important I want to talk to you about. Can we sit down for a moment?'

They sit on an isolated bench.

Will: 'I don't know where to start really. I don't want us to have a row but I've been thinking a lot about us and the future. Basically, I can't take any more of your drinking, Sandy, and I want to ask you to commit yourself to treatment. Otherwise ... '

Sandy: 'Otherwise what ... ?'

Will: 'Otherwise, I think it's time for me to go ... '

Sandy (defensively): 'Jesus, Will, why do you always have to start on this? Go then. I've told you I'm not an alcoholic. I may overdo it occasionally but that's all. I can't believe you're threatening me like this ...'

Will: 'I'm not threatening you ...' (His voice tails off.)

This is very difficult territory to negotiate. Most of us will react defensively if told we have a 'problem': we feel pushed into a corner and then come out fighting. To avoid the inevitable up/down positioning of the one without the problem (healthy) over the one with are the problem (sick), Will has to speak from his heart more than his head. He loves Sandy a lot so it's a question of communicating this truth. Here's Practice 2.

▶ **PRACTICE 2**

Will: 'Can we sit down for a moment? I want to talk about something.'

They sit down.

Will: '*Sandy . . .* '(He looks at her directly.) '*I don't know how to say this but I feel utterly helpless. I see you drinking too much for your own good*' (She bristles.) '*Well, I know that's my opinion but I don't want to quarrel about whether you're an alcoholic or not. That's not the point. The point is I can't bear watching you drink as much as you do.*'

Sandy: 'It doesn't do me any harm.'

Will: '*I know you say that and I suppose you have every right to drink yourself to death if you want . . .* '

Sandy laughs: 'You don't have to be so dramatic, Will.'

Will: '*It's not funny, Sandy, it's not fun for me. I love you, I really do, but I cannot bear to be around you when you're drunk. I keep hoping you'll do something about it because I don't want to lose you. But you won't . . . so I can't go on any more.*'

Sandy (suddenly realising the seriousness of what Will is saying): 'What are you saying, Will? Are you saying, it's all over?'

Will pauses: '*I think I am, Sandy. I think I am. I'm really sorry but I've had enough.*'

We can leave the dialogue there because Will has faced up to a painful communication, for him and for Sandy. He kept hoping against hope that Sandy would eventually 'see the light' and deal with her problem so he wouldn't have to face the grief of separation. He hadn't planned to announce that he wanted to end the relationship but this truth more or less emerged in the dialogue. This often happens.

Once we have the right kind of space in which to be honest with each other, especially in an intimate relationship, we become more acutely aware of what is really going on, of what we are truthfully wanting to say. It isn't always a painful truth but it is always something we find it difficult to say – even 'I love you' can be difficult at times – so it helps to create a blame-free, caring and reciprocal climate in which important things can be said.

Louise and Martin

Louise has a different but equally heartbreaking situation to face. Her husband of 30 years, Martin, has developed Parkinson's disease and his condition has deteriorated over the last three years. Both their sons are grown up and live quite far away and, despite their moral support, Louise has been coping with the increasing burden of care as well as teaching full time in a sixth form college.

She can barely bring herself to admit how resentful she feels towards Martin because, of course, nothing is his fault! Yet, she is exhausted and needing time off but most of all, it is the emotional burden that overwhelms her. Whenever she tries to talk to him, he refuses to discuss his illness. He will not enter into any discussion and although she understands why, she is getting increasingly desperate.

Louise decides to have another go at initiating a discussion. They are both sitting in the garden late in the morning. Her three answers are:

- Martin won't talk about anything

- I am getting desperate

- I want us to have a proper discussion about the future

Louise: 'Martin, we really have to talk about, you know, your illness and what's going to happen.'

Martin says nothing. Looks at the garden.

Louise: 'Martin, did you hear what I said?'

Still no reply.

Louise: 'Martin! Will you answer me?'

Martin, in a quiet and deliberate tone: 'There is absolutely nothing to discuss.'

Louise: 'There is. I want us to talk. I can't bear this silence about everything.'

Martin looks at her angrily: 'What do you *want* me to say, Louise? There is no point in talking. There's nothing to be done about this. You know that!'

Louise feels tears coming into her eyes and goes into the house.

What does Louise want? The answers to her first three questions didn't go far enough. She doesn't only want to talk. When she's more truthful with herself, she realises that part of why she's angry is that she feels trapped. She hasn't been out in months and months, she is either teaching or looking after Martin's needs and she realises that what she really wants is some help. She wants a break. She has come to the end of what she can put up with. This realisation makes her feel dreadful because she feels she should be the totally dutiful wife but she can feel her love for Martin being eroded by her anger and exacerbated by not being able to talk openly. Here's Practice 2.

▶ **PRACTICE 2**

With much more focus (and much more anxiety) Louise has another go.

Louise: 'Martin, I need to talk to you, urgently.'

Martin (alarmed) looks at her, waiting for her to continue.

Louise (a deep breath): 'I love you Martin, I really do and it is really hard to say this but I cannot go on, looking after you without help. I want us to take the time together to talk about how we can manage your illness and needs for the future.'

Martin (taken aback and nervous): 'What do you have in mind?'

Louise: 'I don't know. Perhaps we can look into getting some help but we need to discuss it together. I know you hate to talk about it but I can't bear the silence any more.'

Martin: 'You aren't the one who's ill.'

Louise: 'No, I'm not. But I'm here.'

Martin is quiet and then says: 'Would you rather leave, you know . . . I mean, I couldn't blame you . . .'

Louise: 'Don't be daft.' (Tears come to her eyes but she keeps talking.) 'Oh, Martin. I don't want to leave you. I just want to organise things better, just have a little time off, you know. But I can't do anything unless you are willing to talk to me and tell me what you need and how you're feeling.'

(Time to close.)

Louise goes over and they hold each other. No need for any more words.

Nothing can make some conversations easy given their particular circumstances. We cannot avoid pain at times, as part of loving and living. However, we can avoid the bad taste that's left whenever blame and vindictiveness are the only ground rules for the exchange, when aggression turns the climate into an arena of battle and when fear closes our hearts to the possibility of care.

Chapter Seventeen

Taboo subjects

Some subjects of conversation are in themselves tricky, regardless of whom you are talking to. Such subjects are inherently sensitive because they rouse strong feelings and deeply conflicting values, making us tend to deal with them in a roundabout manner. One such subject is money. Asking for the return of a loan, negotiating a pay rise and settling on a fee for your work when you're self-employed are just a few examples of dialogues that often arise where we have to contend with an issue about which many of us feel uncomfortable in making a direct approach.

The next two scenarios show how the guidelines already described can help when talking about money. The same ground rules apply: taking responsibility for initiating and closing the conversation, considering your three questions in advance and acknowledging your own part in the build-up of a current problem.

Moira and Adam

Moira lent her younger brother Adam a large sum of money a year or so ago to put down as a deposit for a flat. At the time she had some money sitting in a building society and he was looking for a job. She had already begun to find this unpaid loan needling her and then, last week, her mother had mentioned that Adam was planning to go on a safari holiday! That was it!

She now wants to deal with it. Her three answers are:

- Adam hasn't paid me back

- I'm angry

- I'd like him to repay the loan in full

Moira is angry so it will be hard to keep the blame out of it but she's clear what she wants. Her third answer has to be more specific in her mind beforehand. When does she want the loan repaid? Now? Tomorrow? Next week? In instalments? She has to ask herself this before she speaks to Adam. She needs to know, in other words, what is her bottom line and what she is prepared to settle for. She decides that in an ideal world she'd like it all back straightaway but she's prepared to settle for it all to be repaid within a couple of months.

Setting the scene: She arranges to meet him for a drink after work.

The bar is busy. Adam arrives with a workmate, Tom, and Moira briefly considers postponing the discussion and phoning Adam later but then she thinks, what the hell, she's made the effort, and needs to get it over and done with. She asks Tom agreeably if he'd mind leaving them for five minutes because she has something private she needs to talk to her brother about.

This is a sensible move. She wouldn't have a hope of getting this across in front of an audience.

Adam follows her to a quieter corner of the bar.

'What's all that about?' Adam asks.

Moira: 'I needed to talk to you about something in private.'

Adam shakes his head.

Moira takes a breath: 'OK. Look, Adam, you know that money I lent you last year . . .'

Adam: 'Ah, *that's* what this is about. Well, I haven't got it.'

Moira: 'I'd like the money back, Adam. I'd like it back within a month.'

Adam: 'You must be joking. Where am I supposed to get it from?'

Moira (pointedly): 'Well, if you can afford to go on safari . . .'

Oops. We're off into a fight.

To avoid an escalation, Moira will have to take 50/50 responsibility for the situation as it now stands. She is ready to blame her brother for not having the decency to pay it back but when she agreed to the loan, did she stipulate directly and clearly that she wanted the money repaid within a certain time? No, she did not. This means that she cannot blame Adam for not meeting a condition that she herself failed to state.

Taking responsibility will help keep the interaction more equal.

▶ **PRACTICE 2**

Moira: 'Adam, I feel very awkward about asking you but I'd really like to have the money back I lent you.'

Adam (surprised): 'This is a bit sudden! When were you thinking of exactly?'

Moira: 'Well ideally I'd like it back straightaway . . . but, wait a minute, let me finish. In the circumstances, I realise that I never said when I'd like it back so I'm prepared to negotiate.'

Adam: 'What do you need it for now?'

Moira (flummoxed): 'I don't know! Nothing in particular but that's not the point.'

Adam: 'What's the big rush? Look I'm sorry I haven't paid you back but you know you'll get it back some time. I'll pay you when I've got it.'

Crunch time: Moira can give up now because she has no leverage for a fight. Or she can carry on because she wants the loan repaid.

She chooses to carry on.

Moira: 'I know you think I'm being unreasonable but it's bothering me, this loan, Adam. I just want to settle it, you know.'

Adam: 'You are being unreasonable.'

Moira: I'd like us to talk about when you'll pay the money back. Come on, I want to agree on something before Tom comes back. What is going to be reasonable for you?'

Adam: 'I don't know.'

Moira (insistently): 'Adam, please!'

Adam sighs: 'What was it, a thousand, wasn't it?'

Moira: 'Yes, it was. How about two payments?'

Adam: 'Make it three.'

Moira: 'OK. The first one next month, and then the rest over the next two. Can we agree to that?'

Adam: 'I suppose so.'

(Time to close.)

Moira gestures to Tom who comes over.

Moira: 'I'm glad we've sorted it, Adam. Now, do you two want another beer?'

... a context of open negotiation

It takes determination to keep going without the leverage of making someone feel guilty or sorry for you. You need sometimes to remind yourself that you have the right to ask for no other reason than you want to ask. With this right goes the responsibility of making a clear and specific request. It doesn't always mean you'll get what you ask for but if you want to avoid manipulation or coercion, it's the best chance you've got.

Paulette and Jim

Paulette wishes she could be given a pay rise. Her job as office manager has expanded over the two years she's been with the company. Someone left five months ago so she is now doing the job of two people and her responsibilities have grown accordingly. She enjoys her work but is constantly niggled by knowing she should be earning more. This has been fuelled by hearing recently that the new PR manager has started on a higher salary than she has. This information has prompted her to tackle her boss, Jim, the area co-ordinator.

Paulette's three answers are

● I am not being paid enough

● I'm feeling undervalued and fed up

● I'd like an increase

Whenever we take part in a dialogue about money, many women discover a certain reluctance to be specific. The easiest thing in the circumstances is to start off by saying: 'Would it be possible for me to have a pay rise?' or 'I'd like an increase. What do you think?'. These approaches are too general and tentative. We have to learn to be much more specific.

This means often doing a little homework in preparation for making this kind of request: What's the going rate? If we work within a system where we can simply ask to be promoted to another grade of post because this automatically implies a certain financial band, it makes this process easier. Otherwise, we need to find out what we can reasonably ask for, given our qualifications, experience and responsibilities.

This applies also when you are self-employed and having to negotiate a fee for your services or skills. Take the time and trouble to find out what your market value is and then decide what you want. Most of the time we're confounded by our fear of disapproval for asking too much, so we leave the amount blank and hope someone else will fill in the exact figure we have in mind. Taking responsibility includes clearly stating a figure and negotiating from there.

Setting the scene: Taking into account what she knows the new manager is earning and also her own increased responsibilities, Paulette works out that she wants another £7,000.

She makes an appointment beforehand to talk about this with Jim.

Paulette: 'Hi, Jim. Is it OK to come in?'

Jim: 'Sure. Sit down.'

Paulette: 'Jim, I'm basically here because I'd like a pay rise. I was thinking about another £7,000.' (She says this with zero conviction.) *'And I was wondering what you thought.'*

Jim (with a dubious expression on his face): 'Well, it's a bit of a jump. I don't know, Paulette, I don't know whether we can afford to pay you that.'

Paulette: 'You see, with Beryl leaving I am really doing two people's work now.'

Jim: 'Yes, I see that. I just don't know if we have the money though. You know how things are.'

Paulette (using what she imagines is her trump card): 'Well, I happen to know that Kay, you know the new PR manager, started on more than I did so . . .'

Jim (looks uncomfortable): 'I really can't discuss any other employee's salary, Paulette.'

Paulette (feeling very awkward now): 'I was only saying . . . '

Jim: 'I know what you were saying. Look, leave it with me, will you Paulette? I'll have to discuss it with the others. I'll let you know. OK?'

Paulette realises the meeting is over and leaves.

Interestingly, when you use any leverage to boost your own argument it disturbs the equality: instead of the point giving you the advantage, it actually becomes a *dis*advantage. Instead of an equal, one-to-one interaction, Paulette's reference to the other person's salary tips the balance. The person you're speaking to will always feel cornered and then defensiveness will block the channel of communication.

When asking for more money, it's always a much better idea to leave aside comparisons with another person. It's possible to include a general reference to what others in your position might be expected to earn, but avoid direct comparison and stick to building up a strong case as to why you deserve your increase on your *own* merit.

How to leave an inconclusive meeting

A second important lesson for Paulette to learn here is how to leave a meeting that is inconclusive. This often happens. You may have got your request over with clarity and purpose but still the person isn't able to decide on the spot. He or she has to consult with others or needs time to consider. What is important here is that you don't simply leave it open ended. If everything is left in the air, you leave yourself open to continuing uncertainty. You won't know when to ask whether a decision has been made; you'll feel anxious about seeming too impatient and wrecking the chances of a favourable outcome. You'll have needed to summon up your courage to arrange this meeting in the first place and it presumably therefore is important to you, so you need to arrange a different kind of closure.

We need instead to arrange a day or time when we can get back to the person. This provides a boundary to what will otherwise be an anxious time of waiting. So, when you leave the room, make sure you have a firm idea of how long you will have to wait for a reply. Here's Practice 2.

▶ **PRACTICE 2**

Paulette: 'Hi, Jim. Can I come in?'

Jim: 'Sure. Sit down.'

Paulette: 'Jim, I don't find this easy to ask but I've given it a lot of thought and I'd like a salary increase of £7,000.'

Jim's eyes widen in surprise.

Paulette continues: 'The reason I'm asking is because I'm

now doing two people's work – since Beryl left – and I have much more responsibility than when I started. I'm sure you know that.'

Jim: 'Well, yes, I do realise that you're doing more now . . .'

Paulette: 'So that's why I'd like an increase of £7,000.' (She's beginning to find it a bit easier to say this now!) 'What do you think?'

Jim: 'I don't know, Paulette. It's unlikely we can do it for a year or so, you know: things aren't that great at the moment.'

Paulette (avoiding reference to others – leverage – and reinforcing her own merit): 'Well, I'd really like you to consider it, Jim. As I say I've given it a lot of thought and I believe that my work is worth that kind of increase now.'

Jim (taking her seriously): 'I can't give you an answer today, Paulette.'

Paulette: 'I realise that. So, when would you be able to give me an answer? Shall I get back to you, say, next Friday? Would that give you enough time?'

Jim: 'I expect so . . . yes . . . OK next Friday. I should hopefully have an answer for you.'

(Time to close.)

Paulette: 'Fine.' (Stands up.) 'I'll get back to you on Friday then. Bye.'

Paulette leaves with a clear arrangement and if, perchance, Jim hasn't got an answer by Friday, she can repeat the process. She has transformed a passive process of wishing and waiting to an active one of initiative and responsibility.

Mentioning the unmentionable

There are other topics of conversation that we prefer to avoid. How, for example, can you confront someone who suffers from BO? This issue comes up more often than you might expect in a society obsessed with eliminating every trace of smell, wrinkle, hair and other unwanted bodily indication of being a member of the human species.

Understandably, we hesitate to say anything to someone whose smell is offending others. They'll be embarrassed. *You'll* be embarrassed! It's rude to be so personal. What can you ask them to do about it if they can't help it? Whenever an individual has a 'problem' such as BO, it's the easiest thing in the world to see them as ever so slightly inferior: we feel sorry for them. We don't want to go near the problem, even though we'd feel absolutely mortified ourselves to find that we had an offensive problem that nobody was mentioning directly, but that everyone was complaining about behind our backs.

So nobody says anything. And the individual never finds out. You can continue to avoid all these things in life you'd rather not deal with, but if you want to regard the person 'with a problem' as an equal individual, you can make a direct approach using these same guidelines.

Frances and Gerald

Frances is a senior civil servant overseeing a big department and one of the employees has this very problem. Frances is concerned that this man, Gerald, is a sensitive person whom she is sure will be devastated if she says anything. However, it has become a departmental issue in that several other members of staff have refused to share an office with him although nothing obviously has been said directly. Frances decides she can no longer avoid her responsibility to say something to Gerald.

The answers to her three questions are:

- Gerald has a problem with BO

- I don't like it but I feel more concerned about the effect on the staff

- I'd like him to do something to remedy it

Setting the scene: Frances arranges with Gerald to come to her office for the meeting.

Frances: 'Gerald, thank you for coming. Sit down.'

Gerald sits.

Frances: 'I ... em ... I don't know how to begin, Gerald but I'm afraid I have to discuss something extremely delicate with you. I don't know whether you know that you have a problem with body odour ... do you?'

Gerald (gobsmacked): 'You mean ... I smell?!'

Frances: 'Well yes ... I suppose that is what I mean. It's just that some members of staff find it difficult to be in your company and so for the sake of the office, I have to ask you to do something about it.'

Gerald is silent and then says: 'You mean that other people have been complaining ...'

Frances: 'A couple of people have mentioned it, yes ... '

Gerald looks at the floor: 'I don't know what to say.' (He stands up still not looking at Frances.) 'Do you have anything else to speak to me about ... ?'

Frances: 'No, look, Gerald, I really am sorry ...'

Gerald leaves the room feeling humiliated and Frances is left feeling absolutely dreadful.

In her anxiety and her effort to be kind, Frances has made the mistake of diminishing the equality of the two of them as individuals. Yes, he has a problem and yes, she is the boss but it is essential for Frances also to respond as a *person*.

This she can do by being a little more open about her own feelings because then she can be more herself. It is also better to avoid referring to the other members of staff because this immediately changes the dynamic from one to one – Frances to Gerald – to Frances and the whole department versus Gerald, clearly nowhere near equal.

We are often being truthful when we say that 'others have complained' or 'I'm not the only one who thinks so' or 'it's been generally noticed that ...', but as soon as we use these kinds of phrases as leverage for our own argument, we make the whole dynamic unfair. You add ballast to your own argument at the cost of equality. You have to learn to speak for yourself alone.

This also helps because the criticism is coming directly from *you*. Everyone knows that hearing any criticism indirectly, i.e. through a third party, feels much more hurtful and destructive, precisely because there is no opportunity for comeback. The experience of indirect criticism always feels like an attack and is guaranteed to provoke understandable bitterness. Frances must convey this difficult message to Gerald by speaking for *herself*.

▶ **PRACTICE 2**

Frances: 'Gerald, do come in. Take a seat.'

Gerald sits down.

Frances: 'Gerald, I must say this is one of the most difficult things I've ever had to do in this job.' (She looks directly at Gerald.) 'To put it bluntly, Gerald, I have noticed you have a bit of a problem with body odour. Are you aware of that?'

Gerald (shocked): 'No! No one's ever told me that before!'

Frances: 'No, well, it's not an easy thing to say, I can tell you.' (She smiles.)

Gerald (warily): 'Has anyone else said anything?'

Frances: 'Others may have noticed too, Gerald, but the reason I wanted to talk to you now is because I've noticed and I thought that you ought to know because then you can do something about it. I mean, it could be to do with your personal hygiene or it could be your diet, I don't know, but I'm sure you can improve it somehow.'

Gerald is quiet and looks at the floor.

(Time to close.)

Frances (stands up): 'I think it's best we leave it for now, Gerald. I know it's come as a bit of a shock.'

Gerald stands and looks at her: 'Yes, it has. I don't know what to say.'

Frances: 'You don't have to say anything. I do hope you can see I have your best interests at heart. I'm not being unkind. There's just nothing that can make this sort of conversation easy for either of us.'

Gerald moves towards the door and then turns round: 'No . . . no I know that.'

Frances smiles: 'See what you can do. And by the way, don't forget I need the Jenner report by the end of this week. Can you manage that?'

Gerald: 'Oh, yes. I'm almost through with it. There shouldn't be a problem.'

Frances: 'Good. Thanks for coming. Bye.'

What is equal about this interaction, the second time around, is Frances's compassion. Without any gush or artificiality or counselling or pity, her compassion for Gerald as an equal human being shines through the awkwardness of the whole subject. This, more than anything, helps our communication to be equal.

Balancing your status or authority with your feelings as a human being is always a challenge and sometimes has to be addressed in personal relationships as well. Other 'unmentionable' issues arise whenever we make some dreadful and unexpected discovery about someone we care for.

Colin and Jake

Colin is a single parent and has been looking after his son Jake since the death of his wife four years ago. Jake is now 15. Colin is extremely agitated: after Jake had left for school, Colin went into his son's room to rescue the dog that had somehow become shut inside and, to his horror, saw what appeared to be remains of a joint in an ashtray. As he looked around he also found a tiny plastic bag containing a couple of tablets . . . with much worse implications. A whole panoply of feelings are swirling around – shock, guilt, fury, fear. Is he going to wait until Jake comes in from school? What is he going to say? Confront him with the evidence? Colin anticipates a huge row. Feeling very alone with it all, he phones a friend who works in social services for some advice. In this way he gets clearer about what he wants to say:

- I think you're taking drugs

- I'm terrified

- I want you to stop

Setting the scene: Colin decides to talk to Jake later that evening and calls him down from his room.

> Colin: *'Jake, I want to have a serious talk with you.'*

Jake looks mystified.

> Colin: *'Sit down a minute. Look, Jake, this morning I found in your room – I had to go there to let Polly out – what looked like a joint . . . and also some tablets.'*

Jake says nothing but visibly stiffens.

> Colin: *'So what have you got to say?'*

Jake shrugs his shoulders 'Nothing.'

> Colin: *'What do you mean 'nothing'?'*

Jake shrugs his shoulders again.

> Colin: *'Jake, this is serious. I want to know if you're taking drugs.'*

Jake: 'I have a joint occasionally.'

Colin: 'So what are the tablets?'

Jake: 'I don't know.'

Colin: 'What do you mean you don't know? For Christ's sake! Are they Ecstacy? Or what?'

Jake stays silent.

Clearly this is going nowhere. So what's wrong? Again this is hardly a casual situation that can be easily handled. How can Colin engage Jake more effectively?

He's being clear and direct in his questioning but he needs to add another dimension: he has to express his own feelings. Here's Practice 2.

▶ PRACTICE 2

Colin: 'Jake, I want to tell you something very important and I'd like you to listen. This morning I went into your room to rescue Polly and I happened to see the remains of a joint and also some tablets. Jake, look at me. I want you to listen to this.'

Jake looks up reluctantly.

Colin: 'I was completely shocked. I still don't know what to think. I can only imagine the worst ... but I want you to tell me if you're taking drugs and which ones ... look at me, Jake. You have to tell me what's going on.'

Jake: 'There's not much to say.'

Colin: 'Well, whatever you have to say, I want to hear it.

There's no way I can go along with you taking drugs upstairs . . . or anywhere.'

Jake: 'It's only a joint every now and then.'

Colin: 'So what are the tablets for?'

Jake is silent.

Colin: 'I want to know, Jake, please.'

Jake shifts uncomfortably: 'I only take one or two now and then. It's not serious.'

Colin: 'It is serious!' (He stands up and takes a few paces round the room.)

Colin: 'Jake, Jake, Jake! What the hell is happening? Jake, look at me.'

Jake looks up at him.

Colin: 'You know this can't go on. There is no way I'm going to accept you taking drugs. Absolutely no way. I can't just stand round while you do yourself harm.'

Jake: 'It's not that serious. I'm not addicted or anything.'

Colin shakes his head and looks at his son evenly: 'Jake, I love you. I know we've had a rough time these past few years but it doesn't change the fact that I would rather die myself than let you harm yourself in this way.'

Jake is a bit taken aback by his Dad's intensity.

Jake: 'I really don't have a problem, Dad. You're jumping to conclusions.'

Colin: 'If you don't listen to me, I'm going to take you to meet someone who deals with this all the time and who you will listen to.'

Jake looks uncertain.

Colin: 'And if all else fails, Jake, we'll have to involve the police.'

Jake: 'What?!'

Colin: 'Those tablets are illegal, remember, so you're putting me in an awkward position.'

(Time to close.)

Colin: 'Jake, let's stop now. I want you to be absolutely clear about my position and that it won't change. I want you to think about what I've said and we'll talk again tomorrow. OK?'

Jake nods.

Colin: 'I'm going to take Polly out for a quick walk.'

Colin has managed to maintain his parental authority without losing sight of the fact that his son has a choice of response. This is when a communication becomes really powerful but without becoming oppressive.

Chapter Eighteen

One small step

Once you begin to look more honestly at the problem relationships in your life, it then becomes easier to discern a defining link between *past* failure to deal with an issue (while it was small enough to handle) and the seemingly overwhelming situation in the *present*.

Recognising this link is essential, as we've seen, to rein in the tendency to run around dishing out blame. You may, of course, prefer to construct a different mental picture: one that represents you as hapless victims of malign forces (in others) leaving you utterly powerless to alter the course of your fate. There is some comfort in this: you need never face your anxiety or take responsibility for your behaviour. However, this mindset, as long as it persists, robs you of personal power.

Truly understanding the link between past and present – that through lack of clarity, playing dumb, pretending and denial, you have contributed to the gradual acquisition of a hoard of small grievances – you can actually take charge of your life instead of feeling burdened and out of control. You can take the opportunity to make small changes that have a real and significant impact.

Breda and Alan

Breda feels she is stuck in an impossible situation at work. She is a senior researcher at a large university and the relationship between herself and her supervisor, Alan, has gone from bad to worse over the course of three years. She can list her complaints: he is aggressive, he doesn't listen, he doesn't respect her. In her catalogue of stored complaints, she recounts him ignoring her opinions, belittling her in front of others, failing to give her adequate supervision, even taking credit for a paper that she had produced. Quite a pile!

This isn't unusual. Sometimes you find yourself caught up in what seems a nightmarish relationship with someone. It seems *so* big that you truly feel powerless to deal with it. This is true. As it stands, you can't deal with it. The idea of selecting one manageable pebble to deal with appears futile and pointless. Yet, this is exactly where you actually have to start. It's the only place to start: *one* pebble, *one* small thing you can change. The act of choosing one incident to challenge interrupts the pattern of powerlessness and victimisation. Making one single choice blows that vital breath of air into the flame of personal power.

Breda decides to tackle the incident involving Alan taking the credit for her paper.

This is sensible because – even though embedded in a whole context of disregard and generally abusive behaviour – it represents an individual incident.

Her three answers are:

● Alan sent the paper out via e-mail with his name on it

- I was furious

- I'd like my name to have been there

Setting the scene: Breda finds it hard to know when to talk to Alan. He's not often in his office and, when he is, he's usually busy on his computer. However, as she has no other option, she decides to see him there.

Breda (standing in the doorway to Alan's office): 'Alan, do you have a moment?'

Alan grunts, his eyes still on the screen.

Breda waits a few seconds: 'Alan, do you have a moment?'

Alan: 'What do you want? I'm busy.'

Breda: 'I'd like to talk to you.'

Alan: 'What about?'

Breda: 'I'd like to talk to you about something important.'

Alan: 'Can't it wait?' (Still not looking at her.)

Breda: 'Not really. It's about the research paper last month.'

Alan: 'What about it?'

Breda: 'I want to talk to you about the fact that it didn't have my name on it.'

Alan: 'You're part of the work in this lab.'

Breda: 'I know but I think it should have had my name on it.'

Alan: 'I really haven't got time to talk about this now.'

All this time, Alan's eyes haven't once left the computer screen.

What Breda is doing is staying stuck in her pattern of response. Because of the conviction of powerlessness, she is fixed in that mode of behaviour. Whenever you talk to someone while their eyes and ears are occupied elsewhere, you convey that what you are saying is not worth listening to. Even though you don't actually say this in words, this message comes across to the other person. It's one of the many ways we reduce the effectiveness of what we are trying so hard to communicate: without realising it, we reinforce the impression that what we are saying is not important. This is what Breda needs to change for herself. Even though Alan may not take her seriously, she has to take herself seriously. Here's Practice 2.

▶ **PRACTICE 2**

In this instance, Breda needs to wait until Alan looks at her *before* she speaks. A tiny detail, perhaps, but this is exactly how the interlocking dynamics of 'power over' and 'power under' establish themselves and over time become welded together. If Breda can alter her part in this pattern, it will alter the dynamic of the whole dialogue.

> *Breda (standing in the doorway): 'Alan, I'd like to speak to you.'*

> *Waits ... and waits ... and waits, her anxiety mounting by the second.*

> Alan looks up briefly.

> *Breda: 'I'd like to speak to you.'*

> Alan looks back to the screen: 'What about?'

> *Breda starts to reply then holds her tongue and waits.*

Alan looks up again.

Breda: 'It's something important and will take five minutes of your time.'

Alan (Looks back to the screen): 'Well, what is it?'

Breda again waits, nervous inside but stays silent.

Alan looks up at her: 'What is it?'

Breda (getting into her stride a little): 'I'd like five minutes of your time, Alan. If now is not convenient will you tell me when it will be?'

Alan: 'I've got to finish this.'

Breda: 'I know you're busy but I'd like to talk to you today. It's important.' (She's starting to take herself seriously despite her anxiety.)

Alan lets out a heavy sigh and says grudgingly: 'Well, we can do it now if you want.'

Breda sits down. Alan looks back at the screen. Breda waits. She's finding it easier now.

Alan turns himself round in his chair to face her.

Breda: 'Alan, this isn't easy for me but I want to you to know that when I saw that the last research paper had gone out with your name at the bottom and not mine, I was really upset.'

Alan (surprised): 'Why? What we do is a team effort.'

Breda: 'Yes, Alan but it was my research, my work, you know it was, and I was ... angry that it didn't have my name anywhere to reflect that.'

Alan mutters: 'I'm sure there's a perfectly good explanation. You don't have to take it personally.'

Breda: 'I do take it personally because it was my work. In future I'd like you to make sure that if my work is published, my name is on it. Could you agree to that?'

Alan (taken aback but not defensive): 'I suppose so. As I said, you don't have to take it personally.'

Breda: 'All I'm asking for is that in future my work is properly acknowledged.'

(Essential to get out quickly now and close.)

Breda gets up and goes towards the door: 'Thanks for your time, Alan. I won't keep you any longer. Bye.' (Exits.)

This is a definite turning point. Although she and Alan will never get on, although nothing can take away her misery of the past three years and although Alan will probably never give her all the credit she deserves, Breda has managed to confront her own powerlessness by dealing with one specific incident. Nothing is ever too small in this sense because it is representative of the whole. Once you choose one thing and confront it, you are by implication confronting the entire pattern. All you need is one thread to start unwinding and change will be set in motion.

Once Breda has experienced having a few options available to her (instead of none), she may decide to confront other incidents in which she felt put down by Alan, using the same guidelines. Possibly, she'll feel more empowered to challenge things as they occur or, if necessary, look for another post. The point to remember is that if you don't ever learn that you have a choice and therefore never learn to speak up, you're likely to move on to another job or another relationship with this unresolved issue inside you: the diminished personal power continues. By challenging Alan and restoring some personal power, Breda has claimed more equality for herself and this she can carry within, into her future.

Sometimes, we find ourselves in a nightmare situation through no fault of our own: we inherit it, for example, as part of taking on a new job. Whenever you're faced with the question of magnitude – How on earth can I tackle something so complex and overwhelming? – remember the principle of taking one small step.

Robert and Roy

Robert started work as a senior editor for a publishing company six months ago. Two editors had been made redundant before he was appointed and this had been resented by several of the remaining employees, some of whom continue to socialise with the two who have left. Robert has tried unsuccessfully to build bridges; his gestures have been roundly rejected, especially by Roy, one of the older editors, with whom Robert has to work quite closely.

The whole situation is too large to address so what can Robert aim for? What does he want? On occasion, when you ask yourself the third question, you may find that it is genuinely impossible to find a specific answer because ill will has built up on both sides. Unexpressed feelings often create an invisible but tangible gulf, affecting the possibility of genuine friendship or, as in this instance, co-operation at work. This is when your third answer need not be so much a specific request as a request for a discussion to clear the air together. This is what Robert decides:

- There's a lot of hostility that interferes with work

- I feel frustrated

- I'd like us to have a proper discussion to clear the air

Setting the scene: He arranges a meeting with Roy in his office.

Robert: 'Roy, good morning. Please sit down.'

Roy sits.

Robert (breathes in deeply): 'Roy, we need to have a talk about things here.'

Roy bristles.

Robert: 'I realise you aren't happy with my being here – you've made this perfectly clear – but we have to find a way of working more effectively together.'

Roy glowers in silence.

Robert: 'You do know what I'm talking about, don't you?'

Roy considers the question: 'I don't believe you have many grounds for accusing me of lack of co-operation.'

Robert: 'I'm not accusing you of anything. I just think we need to sort things out.'

Roy: 'There is nothing to sort out, really, is there? We don't get on: that's just the way it is.'

This sounds like stalemate. Robert is losing his focus by trying to appease too quickly and too vaguely. He also needs to find another opening statement. It is important to challenge the habit of saying 'we' when we are anxious. Many times, when in a position of some authority over someone, an individual will say 'I thought we should have a little chat' or 'We need to speak about what's happening'. In both these examples, the 'we' comes across as manipulative. It tends to make the other person suspicious and defensive because it's an attempt to make things seem cosier than they actually are. The speaker is not taking responsibility for saying '*I* am anxious about this but would like to have to time to talk to you' or '*I* find this difficult but it's important for me to have a conversation about this . . .'. A false 'we' isn't friendly at all: it just comes across as false. Here's Practice 2.

▶ **PRACTICE 2**

Robert: 'Good morning, Roy. Take a seat.'

Roy sits.

Robert: 'Roy, I've asked you in because I'm faced with a difficult situation. I've tried to improve our working relationship but everything I do seems to fail. I'm extremely frustrated by having to contend with your dislike of me, not out of any personal need but because it interferes with us working together. I'd like to take the time to sort things out enough so that we can find a way to move on. What do you think?'

Roy (certainly paying more attention): 'What do you have in mind?'

Robert: 'I don't have anything in mind. I only want to talk more openly. Although you've never said so to me, I imagine you're still resentful about Denis and Bill going.'

Roy: 'They were good people.'

Robert: 'I'm sure they were and I know it's always upsetting when that kind of thing happens.'

Roy (glaring at Robert): 'Being made redundant for no reason at all?'

Robert: 'I don't know the ins and outs of it, Roy: it happened before I came. All I know is that I've been left with the problems. Which is why I want to sort things out with you so we can move on.'

Roy: 'What do you want?'

Robert (looks directly at Roy): 'I'm not issuing orders, Roy. I want you to co-operate so I have to know, first of all, whether you're willing to do so ... from now on.'

(Time to close.)

Robert: 'Have a think about it. Will you?'

Roy gives a little grunt but his surliness has disappeared.

Robert stands: 'In the meantime, will you organise the others for a meeting about the new magazine ... tomorrow some time?'

This is enough. The whole picture, the resentment, the history will remain but Robert has taken a step towards changing one part of it. Settling for what we can change and letting go of what we can't is a very, very important lesson to learn.

Chapter Nineteen

Dealing with harassment

Differentiating between what we can and cannot change often arises as an issue in confrontation. Sometimes we are deterred from speaking up because a certain topic is a sort of no-go area, not because it's embarrassing but because it is too emotive or too heavy. Racism and sexism are two such

... an issue in confrontation

areas. You can't take on the whole system so how do you deal with one issue without getting totally entrenched and way out of your depth? It's easier by far to keep quiet.

The problems get worse as a result. We have legislation in place supposedly to protect us from racial or sexual harassment, which is fine in theory but, as everyone knows, in practice, it's a totally different story. Legislation offers one way, a perpendicular way, of dealing with this kind of harassment. We can store up enough evidence to take our case to a tribunal where complaints can be assessed and individual offenders judged to be guilty or innocent. This involves a lengthy and often costly process, with the complainant often resented for causing 'trouble' even if the outcome is favourable. If you happen to be higher up the ladder in terms of earning power, you may be paid vast amounts of money in compensation claims. But those stories that hit the headlines are a tiny tip of an enormous iceberg of ongoing harassment in professional, educational and social contexts that not only go unreported but are hardly ever challenged.

One of the consequences of legislation is that racism and sexism, though still very much alive and kicking, have gone underground. Instead of having to deal with gross behaviour in the workplace like having your breasts fondled or being called a Paki to your face, we are left caught in the trap of not knowing whether we are *imagining* what is happening. As we've seen, we like to be sure of our ground before confronting anything so this doubt erodes our ability to confront what we believe is going on.

Most harassment at work occurs in the forms of veiled put-downs, exclusion from decision-making, being asked to fulfil demeaning tasks, being denied credit for work you've achieved or having your expertise publicly undermined. Staying trapped in doubt as to the legitimacy (will you be able to prove it?) of what you're feeling undermines your personal power: you're unable to make a move. You feel something happening while being endlessly assured it isn't, so you then feel embarrassed to speak up as if somehow you are personally at fault for daring to mentioning a taboo subject.

So the first step is to stop denying what is going on. It doesn't mean you can change everything; it doesn't mean that you're always right; but it does mean that if you feel uncomfortable about someone's behaviour it's worth considering the validity of your experience. Forget the theory: sexist and racist attitudes are far too deeply entrenched to be eliminated by any act of legislation. Face reality and then decide what to do next.

Though it may be worthwhile taking your complaints to a formal authority as a last resort, it is possible to speak up far more often than we do, on a one-to-one basis, once we know how.

Kavitha and Nathan

Kavitha is a microbiologist in a pharmaceutical firm. Twice in three years there has been the possibility of moving to a higher post and although she has expressed her interest, she believes she has been overlooked. Being Indian she wonders if her colour goes against her.

The same principles apply when confronting sexism or racism as with any other topic. Ask yourself, what is happening? What do you feel? What would you like to be different?

She wants to tell Nathan, her immediate boss with whom she has an uneasy relationship, that:

● I am concerned that I am being overlooked for promotion

● I am disappointed

● I'd like to know what is going on

Setting the scene: Kavitha arranges a meeting with Nathan.

> Kavitha: 'Thank you for seeing me, Nathan, I'd like to talk about why I wasn't considered for the senior research post last month.'
>
> Nathan: 'You were considered but there was someone more qualified.'
>
> Kavitha: 'I'm wondering ... if ... it has anything to do with my nationality.'
>
> Nathan (defensive, looks straight at her): 'I know what you're implying. Don't start accusing me of anything sinister.'
>
> Kavitha: 'I wasn't accusing you, I wondered if there was a possibility ...'
>
> Nathan: 'I really don't have any more time, Kiviti, I have to get on ...'

Now, Kavitha could leave it there. She's not sure and yet ... there are several indications that she is not simply suffering from an overactive imagination. Nathan never gets her name right, he talks across over her in meetings and often grimaces when she's speaking to indicate that he finds it a hugely inconvenient effort to get past her accent. She even checked with her students but they told her they had no difficulty whatsoever in understanding her.

She needs to be more definite ... and equal. Here's Practice 2:

▶ **PRACTICE 2**

Kavitha: 'Nathan, thank you for agreeing to this meeting. I want to discuss something serious with you.' (She sits back in her chair and looks straight at him.) 'Nathan, this is never an easy subject to bring up but I have the feeling that you might be a little prejudiced against me.'

Nathan: 'Don't be ridiculous!'

Kavitha: 'I get the impression that you are uncomfortable with me because I am an Indian woman and not the same nationality as you are.'

Nathan: 'You're talking nonsense, Kiviti.'

Kavitha: 'My name is Ka ... vi ... tha. I don't want to accuse you of anything, Nathan, but I am wondering if my nationality makes you blind to my ability as a scientist.'

Nathan looks unnerved.

Kavitha: 'It happens easily, you know.'

Nathan (warily): 'I really don't know what you mean.'

Kavitha: 'Do you have a problem with any of my work, Nathan?'

Nathan: 'No, not at all.'

Kavitha: 'Are you pleased with my work here? Tell me honestly?'

Nathan: 'Your work is fine.'

Kavitha: 'Then I'd like you to seriously consider me for a promotion when the next opportunity arises. Would you agree to that?'

Nathan (now a bit perplexed): 'Yes, yes, of course, Kiviti . . . I mean, Kavitta.'

Kavitha: 'Kavitha.'

Nathan: 'Sorry . . . Kavitha.'

(Definitely time to close now.)

Kavitha stands and smiles: 'Thank you for your time, Nathan.' (She leaves his office.)

Gentle forcefulness like this is a hallmark of personal power. No guns, no weapons, but a persistent and unwavering conviction in your own perception. The key to confronting sexist and racist issues is to acknowledge what is happening and, *at the same time*, to understand that it is rarely personal. This means that because, for example, your skin isn't white or you are female, you will find yourself the target of residual aggression: intimidation, derision, being discounted or excluded. This is all based in fear and the aggressive need to establish dominance over someone else.

When any of us is afraid and insecure ourselves, we hold on to our own rung of the ladder more tightly and make ourselves feel more secure by looking down. As long as we can insist that there are those down there, we can feel temporarily less anxious about loss of status ourselves. It's the same the world over because of the dominance of the perpendicular system.

It is beyond our own personal remit to sort this out since it is much bigger than any one individual. Therefore, choosing to deal with one small instance of a much wider pattern helps us to balance the personal offence or hurt with a wider awareness that we are part of this whole system. Curiously this makes it easier to avoid accusation and blame. Seeing what is happening in its context means we can then tackle the small part of it that we have to endure instead of getting stuck in the helplessness of feeling personally victimised.

When you balance this, as Kavitha did, you become powerful in a disarming way. You see what is happening and you see the other person themselves trapped in a system. It doesn't mean you continue to collude with it, but it means you can exercise a measure of compassion for the perpetrator too, as an equal human being. This is always the base of personal power and the key to confrontation.

Gail and Ian

If the occasion demands it, confrontation can be more overtly forceful. Anger can be communicated very powerfully without it becoming aggressive.

Gail is gay and although she makes no secret of this, she doesn't go in for wearing 'lusty lesbian' emblazoned across her T-shirt. She prefers to keep discreet boundaries between work and home. She is assistant finance manager in a mobile phone company in a lively open plan office where most of the employees are fairly young. There is typically lots of general banter and, on this particular occasion, there is an argument going on between the male and female employees about the merits of a particular TV personality. One young man, Ian, is a bit of a loudmouth. He is counting up the votes as Gail approaches.

'The guys say yes, the girls say no . . .' he sees Gail. 'What do you say, Gail, I guess you're in between, eh?' with a knowing smile. 'Keeping all your options open.' There is a brief awkward silence before people get back to their screens.

Gail doesn't like Ian's manner. This isn't the first time he's alluded to her being gay, not as a mere comment but always trying to embarrass her. She knows she's not paranoid. One of the obstacles to speaking up in this kind of context is the fear of being accused of having no sense of humour. In our culture, the most common form of humour on stage, television and cinema is to raise a laugh through put-downs, i.e. through indirect aggression. We generate mirth through ridicule, oneupmanship, humiliation, watching someone make a fool of themselves, being 'taken down a peg or two'.

There is little you can do about this except challenge the denial implicit in the defensive statement: 'I was only trying to be funny'. If it hurts, and especially if it is said in front of an audience, you can virtually guarantee that the intention is to make a point, score a goal, get a laugh, i.e. to put you down, thus reinforcing the power of the speaker.

Gail isn't able to come up with a quick response and gets cross with herself. She's convinced that if only she could have thought of a witty reply, she wouldn't have looked stupid in front of everyone. This line of thinking is understandable but misleading. There are many ways of matching one put-down with another, bigger put-down: this is part of our humour. But few of us, when hurt, have the ability to conjure up a scintillating phrase as a counterattack. More crucially, even the wittiest riposte will never facilitate genuine communication. It may be entertaining to an audience but it won't convey to the 'offender' what you feel in a way that can be heard or really taken on board.

Giving up on fantasy, Gail decides to tackle the reality of Ian's comments:

● He was making an indirect comment about my sexuality

- I am outraged

- I'd like him to stop

Setting the scene: She has the sense to call him aside to an unpopulated corner of the office.

> *Gail: 'Ian, could we have a word ... can we go to the meeting room for a moment?'*

> Ian (looking wary): 'OK.'

> *Gail: 'Ian, I really don't appreciate comments like that. I'd be grateful if you didn't do it again. OK?' (Prepares to go.)*

> Ian: 'Hang on! What comment?'

> *Gail: 'You know perfectly well what comment.'*

> Ian: 'It was just a slip, sorry. Didn't know you were so sensitive.'

> *Gail (even more irritated): 'I'm not sensitive, Ian. But I don't appreciate you making comments in front of everyone. OK?'*

> Ian shrugs: 'OK, but you don't have to get so heavy about it.'

Gail is not satisfied because she still feels on the defensive. She'd prefer to speak from a different base. To do this she'll have to express her feelings openly.

Using the word 'appreciate' in this context isn't helpful. It's frequently used when we want to ask someone to stop doing something but it always smacks of slight superiority. It is close to phrases like 'We don't expect that kind of behaviour' or 'Your behaviour leaves much to be desired' and is therefore best avoided if you don't want to make the other person feel instantly like a naughty child.

Gail needs to be more specific about what she feels to enable her to feel more equal and more in charge of the interaction that she has initiated. Here's Practice 2.

▶ PRACTICE 2

Gail: 'Ian, this is very hard for me to say but I was furious when you made that comment in front of everyone.'

Ian 'It slipped out. I didn't mean it.'

Gail (looks at him evenly): 'I'd like you to know, Ian, that I'm proud of my sexuality but that it is private. Here, I am an assistant finance manager, that's all. Do you understand me?'

Ian: (playing misunderstood): 'It was only a laugh.'

Gail (keeps her gaze on him): 'Ian, I don't want any more comments like that. It's not funny to me so pack it in.'

(She says this in an angry tone.)

Ian is silenced by her sudden fierceness. He opens his eyes wide and shrugs his shoulders in response.

(Definitely time to close.)

Gail turns and goes back into the main office having established some clear boundaries: she can put aside her need to be liked by a particular individual and settle for respect instead.

Two incidents, two challenges. Each time we challenge one small part of the whole oppressive system, we feel less of a helpless victim. Harassment of this kind is a pain to have to deal with it but it *is* a very common, though less visible, problem. Perhaps if, as individuals, we spoke up more often and more effectively, it would have far more emotional impact than any piece of legislation.

Chapter Twenty

Rejection

One way or another, rejection is always an issue when we decide to be direct with someone. Fear of being rejected ourselves is at the root of many of those concerns that dissuade us from speaking up. There's also the fear that others will feel rejected. Much of the time, we *imagine* the inevitable rejection someone will feel if we risk being honest and then find it isn't actually as bad as we feared. At other times though, there is no escaping the reality that what we are communicating *is* a definite rejection.

Brenda and Barbara

Brenda and Denis have been going on holiday with Barbara and Bill for over ten years. They get on fine and enjoy their time together but, this time, Denis wants to ring the changes. Brenda feels sympathetic and wouldn't mind a change herself but Barbara is a very old friend from decades ago and she is extremely worried about telling her.

One thing to consider again is the timing. Holidays have to be booked and even though it's January, she knows that Barbara and Bill will be planning their holiday already. The days pass and she puts the off moment. She's even got to the point of dreading the phone ringing in case it's Barbara phoning to talk about the holiday.

Instead of waiting anxiously, Brenda must take the initiative. Her three answers are:

- We usually go on holiday together

- I'm feeling awful

- Because I want to say we're not going this year

It's important that Brenda is in agreement with Denis over this issue: otherwise it would be more difficult, communicating a decision on someone else's behalf, but in this case, she is clear that he would like a change as well. After thinking through her third answer carefully, she's clear that the decision is not that they never want to go on holiday together again: at the moment, they just don't know.

Setting the scene: She decides to phone Barbara.

Brenda: 'Hello, Barbara? It's Brenda.'

Barbara: 'I was just going to ring you! How are you doing?'

Brenda: 'Fine. Did you have a good Christmas?'

Barbara: 'Yes, the grandchildren were all here for two days. Hectic but fun.'

Brenda: 'I bet. We went to a hotel.'

Barbara: 'Did you? How relaxing . . . where was it?'

Hang on a minute ... when is Brenda going to start?

This is yet another common mistake we make at the start of any difficult conversation – on the phone or face to face – is trying to staunch the anxiety with a lot of chitchat.

It's easy to spot openings like this.

You dread having to give someone a criticism so you start with: 'Morning, Marjorie' (in a suitably bright and cheerful voice.) 'Lovely morning, isn't it? Did you have a nice weekend?'

Or: 'Now Marjorie, you know how *much* your work is appreciated here and how *much* we value your contribution ... '

Avoid chit chat. A simple 'Good morning' or 'Hello' is sufficient to be polite.

The reason for this is that your anxiety is going to continue to rise unabated as you continue to put off the moment, which won't help once you start. Also, you're assuming the other person is stupid. In fact, they are more than likely to sense that something is amiss and their tension levels will rise as well.

Remember, once you start, not to put it off for ever but jump in and express your feelings openly instead.

Brenda: 'Hello, Barbara?'

Barbara: 'How funny! I was just going to call you! How is everything?'

Brenda: 'Barbara, before we go on, I've got to say something.'

Barbara: 'Whatever's wrong?'

Brenda: 'Nothing's wrong. Well, that's not true. Look, (takes a breath)' Barbara, I feel awful about this but Denis and I have been thinking that perhaps this year, we might go on holiday, you know, apart. Not with you and Bill.'

Barbara (after a silence): 'Why?'

Brenda: 'No reason really, we just thought that we'd like a change this year.'

Barbara: 'So we might go together next year?'

Brenda: 'I don't know. We haven't thought that far ahead.'

Barbara: 'I'm really disappointed. We've always had such a good time ... or didn't you enjoy it?'

Brenda: 'No, I did. We did. It's just that we thought we'd like a change. I do feel terrible about this, Barbara. I don't want it to spoil things between us, you know.'

Barbara is sad but resigned.

(When you reject someone, and you've said what you have to say, it's important to allow for the other person's response: you can do this without being intrusive.)

Brenda: 'I'm sorry to tell you like this. Do you hate me now?'

Barbara: 'No, 'course I don't. I'm sad, though ... And surprised, I suppose. I'm still wondering what I've done wrong. Or whether I missed something.'

Brenda: 'There isn't anything wrong, I promise. It's only that Denis felt like a change and I agreed it might be a good idea ... that's all. I've been dreading telling you.'

Barbara: 'OK then.' (Silence.)

(Time for Brenda to close the conversation.)

Brenda: 'I'm wondering if we could meet soon? Even if we can't all four of us get together, can you and I meet? We could go up to London or something. I'd like to catch up with everything.'

Barbara: 'Maybe when the weather's a bit warmer.'

Brenda: 'I don't want to leave it too long. Can we make it in March?'

Barbara: ' That sounds fine.'

Brenda: ' I'd like that . . . I'll phone you again. Bye for now.'

There may be an awkwardness but a firm friendship can survive such decisions communicated in this way. Brenda will have to wait and see. She's been honest and indicated her willingness to meet Barbara. She can only take one step at a time. And you never know, sometimes things turn out differently than you imagine. It's not impossible that Barbara and Bill could themselves have been feeling stuck in the arrangement. Perhaps this decision will be a catalyst. We don't know and can't control it. All we can control is our communication.

Ellie and Ted

Telling someone you don't want to go out with them also presents us with the inevitability of rejection. Ellie is at college. She's been out with Ted a couple of times for a drink but feels uncomfortable in some way. He's quite nice but she's aware that he is much keener than she is and also seems to have something much more long term in mind than she does herself. She finds herself avoiding him at college and really wants to deal with things more directly. One obstacle is that he's not that attractive and she feels a bit sorry for him.

Feeling sorry for someone is part of a familiar power dynamic. If you're attractive then you're higher up the scale than if you're not. So if you're attractive then you feel up there: if you're not, the reverse. Feeling sorry for someone has little to do with care or compassion and has nothing to do with equality. Not being honest or trying to let someone down gently because you feel sorry for someone can never be equal. Feeling sorry means you see the other person on a lower rung. Always.

Ellie decides she wants to be more up front and direct. She could wait until Ted next approaches her but she chooses to take the initiative and seek him out.

Her three answers are clear cut:

- I've been out with Ted a few times

- I feel uncomfortable

- I don't want to go out with him any more

Setting the scene: She goes to a class where she knows she'll find him and waits. Ted comes out of the room and smiles on seeing her there.

Ted: 'Hi! Nice to see you!'

Ellie: 'Can we talk privately somewhere? We could go outside.'

(Ted's a bit mystified but follows Ellie out to where they can sit down.)

Ellie: 'Ted, there's something I want to say, but I don't know how to say it.'

Ted looks at her: 'What!?'

Ellie: 'I don't want to go out with you again, just the two of us. Is that OK?' (Bites her lip and feel very awkward.)

Ted looks crestfallen: 'What's the matter? I thought we got on really well together.'

Ellie: 'Well, I suppose we did but I don't feel ... like a commitment right now.'

Ted: 'I've never pressurised you. I don't know what you're talking about.'

Ellie (feeling sorry for him): 'Oh, Ted, I'm sure it'll work out for you ... with someone ...'

Ted feels embarrassed: 'Just leave it, Ellie. See you around.' (He gets up and walks off.)

Ellie needs to stop seeing him as 'poor' Ted because, as long as she does, it'll come across in her tone of voice. Also she must bring the conversation to an end very clearly for both their sakes.

Making room for the other person's response

Whenever you are rejecting someone, the equality of the interaction depends on you allowing someone to express their feelings in response to your announcement. This means

... without you having to mend it

allowing them to state their disappointment or anger without you having to mend it, make it better or wipe it all away. All you have to do is acknowledge it.

The obsession with needing a happy ending for ourselves – so that we don't have to suffer any discomfort – makes us either avoid the response or intrude too far into what is a vital (and private) space for the other person. When any of us feels badly rejected, we need that time and privacy to mend, to put ourselves back together again.

This is often an uncomfortable experience, but, after all, the other person's feelings are in response to your statement. Surviving that discomfort is a challenge. Extremes are easier: either close down your own heart and ignore what the other person is feeling or take total and guilt-ridden responsibility for causing it. The truth is there are times when you need to make difficult priorities and take awkward decisions: in so doing, you'll cause hurt and disappointment and frustration to others. All you can do is honour the other person, by neither protecting them from the truth nor shielding yourself from the consequences. Here's Practice 2.

▶ **PRACTICE 2**

Ellie: 'Ted, there's something I want to say. It's really, really hard but I've decided that I don't want to go out with you any more.'

Ted: 'Why not? I thought we had a good time together.'

Ellie: 'I don't feel strongly enough to go on, that's all. I don't want to get into a serious relationship at the moment. And I wanted to be straight with you instead of trying to avoid you in college.'

Ted: 'I'm really gutted.'

Ellie (breathes in): 'It's hard, Ted. I don't want to hurt you but I'm just being honest, you know.'

Ted (nods slowly): 'Yes, you are certainly being honest!'

(Time to close.)

Ellie stands up: 'I ought to go now. I've got a class soon. Sorry about this, Ted. See you around.' (Goes off.)

Clear, clean and with care: Ellie has been true to herself without putting Ted down in any way.

Rejection is, of couse, an issue at work too. The wish to remain within a rigid comfort zone underlies the expectation that, at work, people should simply cope with rejection and get on with it: no time for feelings. This is the 'hit and run' approach in evidence again. It is why people are informed so clumsily about their failure to be appointed or the rejection of their application, that is, if they get a reply at all. It is possible, however, to make even legitimate rejection – within a hierarchical system – a constructive experience.

Ranjit and Lucy

Ranjit has to tell a junior employee, Lucy, of the decision not to give her a permanent position in charge of website development in the IT company in which he is head of department. This is made more difficult because, six months ago, Lucy was temporarily promoted to this position: although she has met all her deadlines and done a good job, the panel decided her teambuilding skills were not good enough.

His goals are straightforward:

- Lucy has been turned down
- I feel awkward about telling her
- But it's my job to give her the news

Even when, as in this instance, the three answers seem too obvious to bother with, it always helps to have an idea of the answer to the second question: this is what will help you communicate from an internally stronger standpoint.

> *Ranjit: 'Lucy, thanks for coming in.' (Looking away from her.) 'Look, basically, I'm afraid I have to tell you that you haven't got the job.'*
>
> Lucy: 'You're not serious. I thought I'd done really well. Why not?'
>
> *Ranjit: 'Em, everyone felt your teambuilding skills let you down.'*
>
> Lucy (eyes filling with tears): 'That's so unfair. I don't even know what that means.'
>
> *Ranjit (disconcerted) nods and looks into the middle distance, without knowing what to say: 'Anyway, I'm sorry.'*
>
> (Shrugs his shoulders and hopes Lucy will leave very soon.)

It only needs a little more effort on Ranjit's part to make this more human. Here's Practice 2.

▶ **PRACTICE 2**

Ranjit: 'Lucy, thanks for coming in.' (Pauses. Looks at her directly.) *'This is very hard for me, Lucy, but I have to tell you that you didn't get the job.'*

Lucy: 'Oh no! Why not? I thought I'd done really well.'

Ranjit: 'You have in some ways. You've met the deadlines and that's been great but what went against you is lack of teambuilding skills.'

Lucy: 'What does that mean exactly?'

Ranjit: 'It means you need to learn to be more approachable and to consult with others more, as well as managing your responsibility.'

Lucy: 'And how're you supposed to learn that?'

Ranjit: 'Well, you can go on courses.'

Lucy: 'I'm really disappointed.' (Her eyes fill with tears.) 'Sorry.' (Reaches for a tissue.)

Ranjit (not looking away): 'There's no need to apologise. I'm sure you must be really disappointed. You worked hard . . .'

Lucy: 'Pity nobody told me about my lack of skills before.'

Ranjit sighs sympathetically: 'I guess you haven't really had a proper appraisal yet. In principle, there's no reason why you shouldn't apply to do a course. You may find it helpful.'

(Time to close.)

Ranjit: 'We'd both better get back to work now.'

(Lucy nods and gets to her feet.)

Ranjit: 'Thanks for coming in.'

(Lucy leaves.)

Ranjit has managed to deliver bad news with a balance of precision and care.

Chapter Twenty-One

The habit of personal power

What is exciting about the approach described in this book and illustrated in each of the scenarios is that, with practice, you can develop the habit of personal power. By way of summing up, below are some reminders of what behaviour is related to this different kind of confidence.

Acknowledging the truth

Remember that denial leaves us in a fix because congruence – being all of a piece – is not possible. If you're anxious but pretending to be confident, if you feel uncomfortable with what's happening but smile as though you're happy, if you disagree but continue to nod in agreement, if you feel apprehension but ignore it, you are not acknowledging the truth of your experience. Even if you can do nothing about what is happening, once you stop pretending to yourself – 'I don't like what's happening and I'm not prepared to go along with it any more' – the flame receives a breath of air.

Facing and managing anxiety

This follows on from acknowledgement. Most of us try all the time to pretend we're not anxious because we believe it reflects badly on ourselves in terms of maintaining a 'powerful' persona. Accommodating and working through anxiety will always be a crucial aspect of managing difficult situations, helping us survive our initial dread and keep going.

Learning to express and communicate feelings

Once you include emotion as equally relevant to your life as your intellect, you can understand a lot more about your own response to other people's behaviour and therefore take more responsibility for your feelings instead of shifting the blame on to everyone else. Getting clear about your feelings – when they're appropriate, when they're an over-reaction – enables you to put them into words more clearly.

Learning to disagree without a fight

This is one of the hardest lessons in coming to terms with equality: ultimately everyone has the right to their opinions, however deeply you disagree with them. Considering yourself so much more enlightened than others always entails an 'I'm right'/'You're wrong' approach. There's then bound to be a fight and if you happen to be less articulate under pressure, you'll 'lose' and end up feeling unheard. If you simply keep quiet and pretend to go along with the majority view, your sense of your own value plummets. Learning to 'agree to disagree' openly allows you to live with respect for difference.

Challenging unfair criticism

This is a particular aspect of disagreement. It's easy, for example, to let critical comments stick when you could challenge what has been said or implied. You can disagree with what is said while still keeping the door of communication open to what the other person is saying. This helps build a personal boundary that's stronger and also flexible.

Setting limits

A boundary communicates where you begin and where you end. Setting limits means saying 'no', 'stop', 'enough', 'too far' in a way that conveys that you mean it. Failing to do this means handing your power over to others. Finding your personal, physical and emotional boundaries is something you can only do for yourself.

Being clearer about your boundaries helps towards emotional independence. This doesn't mean indifference, far from it, but it describes the ability to allow others their feelings, for example, without always taking responsibility for them. It helps you withstand a measure of disapproval without going to pieces. It helps to survive silences and awkwardness without always having to jump in and fill the silences or try to smooth things over when what is really needed is the time and space for something to evolve more naturally.

Taking the initiative

Taking the first step instead of waiting provides a huge boost to personal power. It is a real tonic to the soul: instead of creeping about, fretting, worrying, avoiding the phone call, anticipating an encounter with dread, take the initiative, face the fear and make the first move.

Making a choice

There's a lot we have no control over in our lives but we do have a great deal of choice in how we choose to relate to all the other people in our lives. The freedom that comes from the realisation of choice also relieves us from the restriction of compulsion. Once you exercise choice in some areas of your life, you find yourself able to do all those things that you really have to do with better grace and less resentment.

Part 3

The way forward

Chapter Twenty-Two

Everyday options

With practice, the experience of personal power becomes more familiar. There will always be times in our lives when, for one reason or another, we won't address issues as they occur but will put off saying anything and consequently end up with an aggravated situation. If you want to handle this effectively, you'll still need to think through your aims beforehand. However, the habit of personal power means that, more and more, you can put the same principles into practice in any situation as it is happening. Whatever external authority you have at the time can be complemented by personal power: if you don't have any authority at that moment, you can always access your personal power. How? By answering those same three questions: What is happening? How do I feel about it? What do I want to be different?

What follows are some cameos of ordinary situations in people's lives. Instead of going into each one in depth, with relevant practices to adjust and improve, there will only be a single interaction. Each small piece of dialogue illustrates that whenever you consider putting anything into words, you have a choice of how and when to do this. Choosing therefore to communicate from a habit of personal power instead of resignation or aggression will always make a difference.

The situations

It's 8 o'clock, Wednesday morning. Amy's received a letter in the morning post. Her friend Laura has written inviting her to go out to Australia for a month at Christmas. Amy is thrilled and then her heart sinks. What will she do about her father? Since her mother died three years ago, he's been quite depressed and depends on Amy's visits, especially at Christmas. She sets off for work preoccupied and in an agony of indecision.

Elsewhere at 10 a.m., Carol is sitting in a meeting with Lisa and Shantosh. All three women are branch managers for an insurance company and meet once a month to exchange ideas and discuss problems before submitting a report. As ever, Lisa and Shantosh are talking to each other as if Carol weren't there.

11.30 a.m. Andy is seething. Brian, his direct boss, has once again failed to turn up for their meeting, scheduled one hour earlier. Andy could have been out visiting a client but arranged to be here and has therefore wasted an entire morning. *Again*. He wants to sort this out once and for all.

1.30 p.m. Usha is having a quick lunch with her mother. Her mother is once again going on about the problem of Usha working instead of staying at home and looking after the children full time. Usha's fed up with it.

4 p.m. Judith is in another meeting, watching the hands of the clock. The Dean is droning on and everyone is looking bored – because they are. She's wishing he'd shut up.

8 p.m. Bridget is washing up after supper. The children are

213

in bed. Her husband, Eddie, is watching TV. He's just told her he's been invited to go to a car rally for the weekend. She didn't give much of a response but everything's churning inside her: she'd assumed they'd spend the weekend together as a family. Now she's trying to work out what to do.

The responses

Every day, we're presented with minor or major tangles in our lives. Each time we face the task of communicating to someone about a difficult topic where we anticipate some kind of conflict, we can decide how to do this.

Amy could let the agony drag on for ages. Or she can ask herself those three questions. When she does this, she realises that she isn't undecided: she's made up her mind. She wants to go to Australia, so how does she tell her father?

Honestly and directly. She phones during a break at work.

Amy: 'Dad. Yes, it's me. I know. I'm at work but I wanted to talk to you about something very important. I had a letter from Laura this morning and well, she's asked me to go over for Christmas.'

Dad: 'Christmas!'

Amy: 'Yes, I know, Dad. I feel dreadful because I'd like to be with you as well but I really want to go to Australia. Would you manage?'

Dad (quietly): 'I don't know . . .'

(Time to close.)

Amy: 'Look, Dad, I can't talk long now. I wanted to let you know so you could have a think. I'll ring you tonight when

I've more time and we can talk about it then. Is that OK?'

Dad: 'All right. Ring me after 8.'

Amy: 'Bye, Dad. Love you. Talk to you tonight.' (Ends the call.)

Carol realises she has an option of keeping quiet and letting the other two do all the talking as usual or she could speak up.

Carol: 'Em, I want to say something.' (The others look at her but carry on talking.) 'I want to say something.' (She uses a firmer tone of voice this time.) 'Look, I know this may sound silly but whenever we meet, you two end up doing all the talking. I know I let it happen but I don't find it easy to interrupt you.'

Shantosh: 'Just say something. Nobody's stopping you.'

Lisa: 'I suppose we do go on a bit, don't we? Sorry. Didn't realise.'

Carol: 'You don't need to apologise. It's up to me to speak up, which is why I am saying something now. Do you think we could agree on some kind of structure for part of our meeting so that we each get a chance to contribute?'

Meanwhile Andy is still fuming. Brian has phoned to say he'll be back in a few minutes. What are Andy's options? He could tackle Brian the minute he walks through the door. If he does so, he'll be unable to avoid an attack, which could have repercussions on their relationship. As with any extreme of emotion, he has an option to cool down first and then speak to Brian as soon as he can get a little emotional distance. He chooses the latter option.

Brian walks in with a couple of colleagues: 'Sorry, Andy. Got caught up again, you know how it is ...'

Andy: 'Brian, I'd like to have five minutes with you, say, at 12.'

Brian: 'We're going to lunch. What do you want to talk about?'

Andy: 'It will wait until 12. Can we make it 12 then, before you go to lunch?'

Brian: 'OK, if it's only a few minutes.'

The scene is set to give Andy the best chance of avoiding aggression.

What does he want? Brian to be on time. Realistic? Andy will settle for an agreement to let him know if their meeting's going to be cancelled.

12.15 p.m., Andy: 'Brian, when you cancel our meetings without telling me, it drives me nuts. I'm left twiddling my thumbs which is not a productive way to use my time.'

Brian: 'I know. I thought Marion would phone you. I'm sorry but I'm under a lot of pressure. You know how it is. Nothing I can do about it.'

Andy: 'Well, what I'd like is that you get a message to me if you're going to be late. Otherwise I'll assume we're not meeting and get on with something else. Can we agree on that?'

Brian: 'Sounds OK.'

Andy: 'Great. That's it then. Have a good lunch.'

Lunch is not going too well for Usha. Her mother has already made her first little dig about her daughter's incompetence as a mother! Usha can keep quiet and wait until she is really exploding under pressure or she can speak while she has a chance of handling it.

> *Usha: 'Mummy, there's something I want to say.' (She looks at her mother.) 'This is not easy because it goes very close to the bone.'*

Mother is fully attentive.

> *Usha: 'I know you disapprove of my working ...'*

Mother: 'It's not that I disapprove ...'

> *Usha: 'Hear me out, Mummy. When you make comments about the fact that I should be at home, it makes me feel dreadful.'*

Mother: 'I'm only worrying for your children.'

> *Usha: 'So do I! It was a big decision to go back to work. I am balancing things, we're both balancing work and family and, I promise you, we may have to reconsider if it appears the kids will suffer. At the moment, though, I'd like your support not your criticism.'*

Mother: 'Well, I do try and support you ... but I take your point, dear.'

> *Usha smiles: 'Thanks. Now, have we got time for a dessert? I hope so!'*

The meeting seems interminable. Judith ponders her own options. She can simply sit it out as usual. But what if she were to say something? Can she really dare challenge the Dean?

217

What does she want? She'd like him to stop droning on and let others talk.

What does she feel? Frustrated.

She is nervous but manages to open her mouth:

Judith: *'Excuse me, em, Professor Wilson. Excuse me.'*

Everyone jolts out of their stupor and stares at her.

Judith: *'I feel awkward interrupting you, but I'm finding myself frustrated because none of us is really taking part in this meeting and I'm wondering if you would ask us to contribute as well? I don't know if anyone agrees with me?'*

She hears a couple of murmurs of agreement.

Judith: *'Professor Wilson, could we share some of our own views about the topic? Would that be possible?'*

Professor Wilson (surprised but not particularly bothered): *'Well, em, yes, why not . . .'*

When she can't find anything else to do in the kitchen, Bridget sits down and thinks. She's clear enough to know that she's beginning to resent Eddie's ability to get out and enjoy himself. She could say nothing and settle into the martyr role. She could then feel cheated and build up lots of resentment. Or she could nip it in the bud.

What does she want? She wants to see how to share the problem more with Eddie.

She goes in and asks to talk after the news has finished. Eddie tells her it's almost over and turns it off.

He pats the sofa for her to come and sit down. She does so but keeps a space between them so she can face him.

Bridget: 'Eddie, I can feel trouble brewing and I want to talk it through.'

Eddie: 'What is it?'

Bridget: 'When you said you were going off on Saturday, I felt pissed off because it feels unfair.'

Eddie: 'Only one day. We're going to your parents on Sunday.'

Bridget: 'I know. I don't begrudge you time off, you need it after working so hard. But I don't know how to manage the chores that I'd imagined we'd do together on Saturday. I don't ever get around to time off for myself.'

Eddie: 'I've never objected to you doing anything.'

Bridget: 'No, you haven't. Look, we're in this together. We talked about this as a co-venture when we decided both to work and bring up a family and I don't want us to stop talking. I don't want to get into the trap of doing all the chores and then resenting your free time. I just don't want to go there.'

Eddie: 'You don't do all the chores.'

Bridget: 'Well, they mostly get done at the weekend, that's the point.'

Eddie: 'So what do you want?'

Bridget: 'It's hard what we're doing. It's hard on both of us. I'd like us to reach a clear agreement about who does what and stick to it.'

Eddie: 'Are you willing to compromise on when it's done,

rather than always on the day you've designated?!'

Bridget (smiling with recognition): 'OK.' (She proffers her hand to shake on it.)

He takes her hand and pulls her towards him.

Chapter Twenty-Three

Saying thank you

So far, issues that are difficult for us have all been something of a more or less unpleasant nature. However, many of us find it difficult even to say anything positive. The result of self-censorship means that many of us regret not having thanked someone properly, told them how much they meant to us or how special they were in our lives, while they were still alive, living near by, sharing the same office, playing in the same team or studying on the same course. We leave it too late, wishing we'd spoken up but not knowing how to at the time.

It goes back to the difficulty in being direct. The ladder spoils our spontaneity. It makes us feel that praising our own manager or telling a teacher how much we've gained from her course is putting ourselves in a 'lower' position. And when we think about offering a compliment, we don't want to appear patronising or as if we're toadying and currying favour. We're also aware that flattery is used to manipulate and coerce, so that on the receiving end of admiration, we get suspicious about the intention behind it: what's he after?

There is a lot of insincere stuff out there, a lot of fake positive 'feedback' and 'let's appreciate each other'. While some people consider this practice as key to getting maximum co-operation from their employees or creating an appropriate climate for a therapeutic group, many of us reject the artificiality. It becomes increasingly difficult in this culture to distinguish real feeling from mere sentiment.

Young children have that disarming ability to express their love with complete innocence and simplicity. As adults, we want to make lavish presentations or demonstrate our love through spending power and we lose the art of simple expression.

We end up getting embarrassed about using our own words, imagining they have to be flowery, although, in terms of impact, a couple of honest, mumbled words from the heart come across as more heartfelt than purchased lines of mass marketed sentimental verse.

We tell ourselves that so and so knows we love them, so why should we bother to risk making a fool of ourselves and say something? Everyone would be embarrassed so we wait until we're caught up in major emotional events like weddings and funerals before we feel we finally have permission to express our feelings.

How we can convey appreciation simply and sincerely? Being specific and expressing your feelings are once again the key to sincerity. Being specific means pushing yourself beyond the generalities of 'You were great' or 'You're doing fine' to specify more precisely what it is you appreciate. This is your gift, after all, and your choice to give it (despite being embarrassed), so it's worth giving some thought and taking a little care about what you genuinely want to thank someone for.

It's also important in these situations to find a closure. All of us tend to feel awkward about getting compliments. So don't worry if the other person looks shy or is even a bit brusque or diffident: it's just our way of handling awkwardness. Say what you want to say and then let the person receive and digest it in their own way: they don't have to make you feel wonderful for taking the risk. Allow any awkwardness and make sure you open and close in the same way as with criticism.

There are no formulas because everyone is different and so what follows are some examples of dialogues that give a flavour of what might be said if we decided to say difficult things directly, when those things are nothing more than genuine compliments or statements of appreciation, respect or love.

Helen has finished three years of art school and wants to thank a particular teacher who's got a bit of a reputation for being grumpy and old-fashioned.

She knocks on his door.

Helen: 'Mr Myers? Can I come in a minute.'

Mr Myers: 'Hello Helen. What can I do for you?'

Helen: 'I've come to see you because I wanted to thank you for your encouragment.'

Mr Myers: 'To do what?'

Helen: 'You've really encouraged me and made me push myself and I've learned such a lot, so thank you.' (Smiles.)

Mr Myers (a bit nonplussed). 'Well, it's er ... it's nice of you to say so.'

Helen hesitates but there is no obvious response: 'Well, I'd better get back now.'

Mr Myers nods. She leaves feeling a bit awkward, but what she doesn't see is the pleasure in the smile on the face of her teacher as she walks away.

Ken and Jill are sitting exhausted on the sofa after everyone has finally left. They've had a first birthday celebration for one of their grandchildren, which has meant a party of some thirteen adults and children all day.

Ken looks over at Jill and smiles: 'Are you happy with the way it all went?'

Jill nodding: 'Yes, I think it went well.'

Ken: 'You know, love, I think we take it for granted a bit, well, I know I do sometimes, but you've worked so hard all day. You've given such a lot. Somehow you manage to be there for everyone and you've done wonderful food and everything just flows.'

Jill (surprised but smiling): 'You do your bit.'

Ken: 'I do my bit, exactly!' (Pauses.) 'You're very special, you know.'

Jill shrugs this off: 'Don't be silly.'

Ken: 'I'm not being silly. Come on, would you like me to make us a cup of tea?'

Anna and her father are having lunch. She hasn't seen her father much since her parents divorced – mainly because of her father's drinking – some years ago. She's arranged to meet him on this occasion to tell him she's going to get engaged.

Dad: 'He sounds very nice. When am I going to meet him?'

Anna: 'I'll bring him over and introduce you. I hope you like him.'

Dad: 'I'm sure I will. If he's good to you and will take care of you, that's all that matters.'

Anna: *'I'm glad you're pleased.'*

Dad: 'Course I am. If you are. You've got a good head on your shoulders and I'm sure you can make the right choice for yourself.'

Anna (pauses): *'Dad, you know, we've had lots of problems and things but I want you to know that I agree with you. I look around at other girls and I sometimes wonder why they get into the relationships they do. I think I'm very lucky to have you as a dad because you've always made me respect myself, you know. You've always said not to worry about what others think too much and not do things just to please other people. That's why I can make up my own mind about things, I'm sure. So, it's all down to you, Dad.'*

Dad (feeling very emotional: can't find any words.)

Anna: *'Oh, Dad.'* (Her eyes fill with tears and she leans over to give him a kiss.) *'Come on, we've got all this food to get through!!'*

Baz and Lawrence are on their way to the park to roller board. They've known each other most of their seventeen years. Lawrence's parents have been splitting up over the last year and it has been very unpleasant and acrimonious. Things are settling down a bit but Lawrence has spent a lot of time with Baz, round at his home, not always talking but when he did, Baz was the only person he trusted.

Lawrence: *'Baz, I feel daft but I want you to know something.'*

Baz (in a singsong voice): 'So, what do you want to tell me?'

Lawrence: *'I just want to say you've been a brilliant mate this year. You really have.'*

Baz (fairly non-committally): 'It's OK'

Lawrence (embarrassed): 'So I wanted to say thanks.'

Baz briefly looks at Lawrence 'It's really OK. I'm sure you'd do the same for me if I was in the same boat.'

Lawrence gets on his board: 'I wouldn't wish that on anyone ... come on, race you to the track ...'

It's impossible to overestimate the value of simple, heartfelt appreciation. Unfortunately discomfort with direct communication means that not only do we avoid criticism but too often, avoid genuine appreciation as well, usually for the only reason that it might cause a little embarrassment or awkwardness. It seems a small price to pay when the risk can pay such huge dividends.

Chapter Twenty-Four

In conclusion

As you become more accustomed to direct communication you find that there is more you can change than you may have thought. It's easy to live under a blanket of conviction that, whatever is happening, you've got to put up with it. A gloomy pall of powerlessness can spread over life and we somehow believe we have to suffer.

Whenever you find yourself putting up with something because you think there is no alternative, try the 'Hetty test'. Hetty is an elderly widow, living in a rural village. Her next- door neighbours, the Clarksons, are charming as indeed is everyone else in the village. Maybe not all charming but there are no real problems. This is why Hetty said nothing for so long.

For 27 years, she has suffered the effects of the Clarksons' oil-fired central heating system. She long ago gave up using her back garden because of the fumes and, even in the front, when the wind is in a particular direction, she cannot mow the grass or do the gardening without being almost overwhelmed by the unpleasant emissions. Not only in winter but also in summer, these fumes have dominated her life.

Why has Hetty said nothing? Because she assumes she has to put up with it. It's just 'fate.' She loves living there and relishes the peace and quiet and the friendliness of her neighbours so has no intention of moving away. Above all, she doesn't say anything because she doesn't want to upset the neighbours: she doesn't want to cause any trouble.

One day, Hetty made a startling discovery. In a chance conversation with a visitor, she learned that although some emission was permanent, it was possible to get the system overhauled and cleaned regularly so that high levels of noxious emissions could be reduced. The discovery that something could be done dramatically transformed Hetty's years of putting up with this problem.

Within two days, she had spoken to the Clarksons who were aghast that she hadn't told them before: they immediately called the company and arranged for a service of the system. Now Hetty wonders why she never said anything before!

The moral of Hetty's story is that whenever you are settling down to a bit of suffering and find yourself saying to yourself 'I've just got to put up with this', ask yourself if that's really true.

There are, of course, times when we can't change things. Earthquakes happen, random violence, accidents, illness, chance meetings: an endless flow of events that disrupt our lives for better or worse. We cannot control a lot of what happens but we do have a choice as to how we respond. The distinction, using this process, between what you can change and what you can't is absolutely vital.

It all hinges on the question: What do you want to be different? Is it something you can reasonably ask for? When it comes to making changes in relationships, we often make the mistake of confusing the two. It is a mistake, for example, to pretend to ask for one specific change from a parent or partner when (if

you're being really honest) you're wishing they were completely different (and better) than they are.

The Wish Fairy

We all have to keep a vigilant eye out for the Wish Fairy. In she
floats bringing with her all kinds of fantasies and daydreams to
tempt us with. She floats past our mental gaze the ideal partner,
the perfect husband, the best colleague in the world, the most
amenable of children, the most efficient and dynamic boss
anyone could hope for . . . but then we wake up!

When you ask yourself what you want to be different and
come up with answers such as:

● I'd like my husband to be more ambitious

● I'd like my boss to be the kind of manager who really under-
stood what teambuilding was all about

. . . all kinds of fantasies and daydreams

- I wish my wife were sexier

- I'd like my boyfriend to notice that things needed doing in the house without my having to point them out

- I'd like my colleague to be more co-operative, like the woman she's replaced

- I'd like my children to be more appreciative

you can detect the seductive persuasions of the Wish Fairy.

Ask yourself again if there is anything specific you could ask for, one small change you could ask the person to make. If you can't come up with anything, don't go any further with this process. Nobody likes to be asked to be a different person. After all, it's a pretty tall order and is likely to provoke a certain amount of aggravation.

Be alert to the Wish Fairy. Once you hear yourself saying 'I'd like you to be more this or more that', you can tell she's around. If you can put her idealism aside and genuinely come up with a request for change, one that the other person can manage, something that you can ask in the current circumstances rather than what you would wish for, then you can proceed.

In summary of the model referred to throughout this book, here are ten tips to remind you what to avoid.

1. Don't attempt to use this process when you are experiencing any extreme emotion – shock, grief, fear, rage. Wait until you have achieved some distance from the situation and your emotional level has diminished to a manageable level.

2. Never begin this process without your answer to the question 'What specifically do I want to be different?'. Have what you'd like clearly in mind beforehand.

3. Don't wait to tackle a problem until it happens again: take the initiative.

4. Don't initiate an important conversation while eating, drinking, making love, watching TV: always, make a separate space and time to talk.

5. Don't initiate a discussion when you bump into someone in the corridor/shop/street. Prearrange to meet beforehand.

6. Never bring in others to back up your opinion as extra leverage; confine yourself to your own feelings and views.

7. Don't let it go on and on: once you've said what you want to say and it has been heard, close.

8. Don't pile on one criticism after another '... and *another* thing ...'. Keep to one item at a time.

9. Keep off the moral high ground: remember to take responsibility when necessary (usually) and keep it equal.

10. Don't ask for the impossible: ask for something that the other person is capable of changing.

Changing the habit of a lifetime

This model is a challenge because it represents for most of us a contradiction to a lifetime's learning. Our learning starts when we experience criticism as very young children. Let's take a simple illustration. A teacher wanting to correct a child's untidy writing in class has different options open to her.

She can say: 'That's a real mess, Sean! Why can't you do it neatly like Barry?'

Or she might choose: 'How many times do I have to tell you,

> *Sean? When I say neatly, I mean neatly!'*

> *Another option: 'You really haven't made enough effort, Sean. You're not going out to play until you get it right.'*

The responsibility to correct is part of her legitimate power and these are three familiar approaches ... all using indirect aggression. Each one indicates that Sean is somehow on a *lower* rung because (a) Barry does better, (b) Sean is too stupid to understand what the teacher really wants or (c) his effort doesn't count so he's threatened with punishment.

If she were to apply the guidelines given in this book, she might say:

> *'I'm not happy with the way you've done that, Sean. I'd like you to rewrite it but this time keep the letters the same size and keep them sitting on the line.'*

All three components – her feelings, current behaviour, and a specific request – are included in that simple response.

You could argue that it doesn't matter as long as she gets a result. However, what a difference it would make if we could start early on to give children a model of criticism and correction that didn't involve putting them *down*.

Why bother?

If, after all this, you're wondering if it's worth it, it's useful to consider the alternatives. We expend a huge amount of time and energy in bitching, complaining and suffering when we could be more dynamic. Grievances add up and up, souring relationships. At work, stored up resentment undermines team potential, reduces effectiveness and maintains people in a constant state of tension instead of creativity.

In our relationships, unexpressed feelings do a lot of harm through eventual aggressive release. So much communication becomes blunted and superficial.

In an age where we can communicate over greater distances more quickly than ever before, we are faced with a parallel inability to be intimate. Words have never been so plentiful and cheap . . . and meaningless. Of course, chatting superficially is normal: we happily talk about fashion, sport, food, gardens, pets, the weather, holidays, new kitchens and so on. It is also normal to experience *feelings*, but in our culture, we equate most feelings with dangerous ground that we need to steer clear of.

The common denominator in every single dialogue in this book, regardless of circumstance or context, is that what makes any interaction difficult is when we experience feelings that we do not know how to express. It's always about feelings.

Our lack of information about feelings and our consequent anxiety and determination to suppress them mean that the easier option – the one we most frequently take – is aggression.

This simple factor accounts for impoverished human relations in every sphere of our lives. When we cannot talk to others honestly, two things happen. We lose the ability to be intimate with one another – with partners, children, friends. We don't know how to say things unless they're superficial. It becomes easier to live out our emotions through identification with characters in TV soaps than to speak up honestly to the person sitting at the next desk or the person beside you in bed!

When we do need to talk about feelings we rely more and more on going to professionals to establish a space where we can put into words things that we cannot say even to those to whom we are closest. Talking in a therapy group or one to one can help but the reason it helps is because it is outside our real lives. No intimacy formed in this artificial atmosphere, however catalytic it may be, can be compared with the bumps and scratches and *work* of real relationships.

Friendship and intimacy are forged through stumbling, acknowledging responsibility, arguing, caring and engaging together. It takes effort and time ... and honesty. We can only achieve genuine, meaningful communication if we are prepared to take the risk of being open and vulnerable with each other. Few people are prepared to do this, to make this effort. Consequently, the Wish Fairy is very much in demand and has difficulty keeping up with our preference for fantasies and stereotyped ideals over the reality of human contact and commitment.

The impact of superficial communication goes far beyond our own personal relationships. It sets the tone for a broader social trend. When we use a process of dialogue as suggested in this book, we actually begin to *listen* to what the other person is saying. If we never mention things or broach difficult issues, we continue to live in our heads. This helps to perpetuate our beliefs that others are basically nasty or unfortunate or mean.

The amazing part of this particular process is that you can discover another side to people. You discover that what you thought about them was wrong. This is what communication is about. You discover they have feelings that you didn't know about and vice versa. As soon as this discovery takes place, it immediately transforms your perception of the other person. You stop seeing the other person as an object, as a thing, a cardboard cut-out, a stereotype. In other words when you speak up, you show you are a person inside and not just a piece of furniture. In a reciprocal dialogue, this will work both ways.

Without real communication shared like this, we will continue to see each other as objects on which to project all sorts of images and imaginings. Whether we revile or adore, disdain or desire, we are all capable of making other people into objects. This is what makes aggression possible. If you see someone else only as a minion, an employee, an au pair, a boss, a child, a Paki, an old man, you restrict them to that label. A one-dimensional label. The whole person becomes reduced to an 'it'. A pretty 'it', a repulsive 'it', a pathetic 'it', a 'fabulous 'it': 'it' is always an object.

On the other hand, genuine communication allows for us to see not only difference but also equality within that difference. I believe the capacity for friendship is the core of all relationships, even in a context of sexual intimacy, because we cannot be friends with anyone other than an equal. While independence represents freedom for some people, the trend towards superficiality encourages emotional isolation and loneliness.

Learning how to make your relationships more real, meaningful and satisfying means taking the risk of direct and honest communication.

The guidelines in this book are like stepping stones across a great swirling river of confrontation, rushing over boulders of interpersonal problems and hidden agendas, hiding sudden deep spots of emotion, as you stand there thinking to yourself: 'How on earth can I get across safely?' The answer is that you step on to one stone and gain a foothold of confidence and self-trust as you keep in sight the far shore. If you don't follow them, you lose your footing but, if you do, you find that, as you gain momentum, you end up almost skipping across because somehow your determination to get there gets the better of the fear with which you started out.

I've witnessed, many thousands of times, individuals who start with trepidation, self-consciously placing one foot after the other on these stones. At some point, something settles.

The words don't seem quite so halting and unfamiliar. We begin to speak with ease, with confidence, with humour. We find our own words, we become more our selves: empty of the force of aggression but full of the energy of personal power.

Once you experience this, you can do it again. You learn to speak up more often at the time instead of postponing. You can take the opportunity to clear up past misunderstandings in relationships, however long ago, by taking equal responsibility and using the guidelines. As your personal power base builds, your eyes open to the reality of other people. Your compassion deepens: the habit of aggression weakens.

Criticism, handled properly, can be a real gift. It's a gift because someone cares enough to make the effort to actually say something to me. This means to me that our relationship matters enough. When we take the risk of communicating difficult things, it means the other person *matters* – it means that living with, working with, being with this person matters enough for you to open up and speak your mind. The enrichment that can come from a renewed understanding between people is surprising but inevitable.

Your own sense of personal power teaches you more clearly when you want to say something and when you choose to keep quiet. Remember the difference between the silence of fear and the silence of wisdom. Above all, you can learn to travel through life less encumbered by unnecessary and imaginary fears. It then becomes easier to open your heart, find your voice and tread lightly!

Index

Index